LOVE AND CONFLICT

GIBSON WINTER is an assistant professor of ethics and society in the Divinity School of the University of Chicago. Ordained to the ministry of the Protestant Episcopal Church, he served as a naval chaplain in the Pacific in World War II, and subsequently returned to Harvard University to earn a Ph.D. in the field of Social Relations. He is widely known for his share in establishing Parishfield, "a training center for laymen to relate Christianity to the industrial and cultural life of America," near Detroit.

LOVE AND CONFLICT

NEW PATTERNS IN FAMILY LIFE

BY

GIBSON WINTER

Dolphin Books
Doubleday & Company, Inc.
Garden City, New York

Love and Conflict was first published
in 1958 by Doubleday & Company, Inc.

Dolphin Books Edition: 1961

TO MY WIFE

For everything there is a season,
and a time for every matter under heaven:
    a time to be born, and a time to die;
    . . .

    a time to embrace, and a time to refrain
    from embracing;
    . . .

    a time to love, and a time to hate. . . .

ECCLESIASTES 3

PREFACE

The family has taken a new lease on life since World War II. The depression and the war seemed to have dealt a mortal blow to the family. Birth rates had dropped. Divorce statistics hit a new high. Returned veterans encountered serious difficulties in adjusting to home life. The most pessimistic predictions about the family were being realized. Such, however, was not to be the fate of the American family. The intense pressures of modern life had established a strong countercurrent. Feelings of personal isolation pressed men and women into an unrelenting search for intimacy. The need for personal intimacy played directly into the hands of the family. The family, now impoverished of many of its traditional tasks, became the exclusive sphere of intimacy in modern life.

Skill in personal intimacy is no easy attainment for a fragile human being. It is particularly difficult for men and women whose lives are absorbed in the competitive struggle of a commercial world. Modern man now finds himself living a double life. He is preoccupied with the achievement of intimate relationships in the home. He is entangled in a multiplicity of impersonal dealings outside the home. This cleavage is reflected in strains within the family. An attempt to understand these strains is the fundamental concern of this book.

A book like this could not be written without the background of painstaking research in family life. Although specific references to this research are not included, the author is indebted to the work of men like Ernest W. Burgess, Carl Zimmerman, Talcott Parsons, R. F. Bales, and others. He is also deeply indebted to the Parishfield Community and its associates. The associations with Francis and Florence Ayres, Olive Robinson, Suzanne de Dietrich, Hugh and Mary White, and the author's own family in that unique community have made a lasting mark on his understanding of personal community. He is indebted to Cynthia Donnelly, Frances Ritsch, and his wife for help with the manuscript. He also owes a debt of gratitude to the many families who shared their personal problems with him and shaped his thinking through their struggles. The personal examples cited in the book are composites of various experiences and represent no identifiable events in particular marriages.

GIBSON WINTER

Federated Theological Faculty
University of Chicago
July 31, 1957

CONTENTS

PREFACE   9

1. EMERGENCE OF THE NEW FAMILY   15
   The Pains of Birth
   Development of the New Family
   The Point of View

2. COLD WAR IN THE FAMILY   31
   Father's Abdication
   Mother Is "All"
   The Mixed Feelings of a Woman
   Why Mother Can't Be "All"
   The Escape from the Home

3. FATHER IN FACT   49
   Male and Female
   Husband and Wife in the Bible
   A New Alliance of Husband and Wife
   Woman's Position in the New Family

4. THE COVENANT OF INTIMACY   71
   Shrinking Man
   The Two Become One
   Separation or Coexistence
   The Make-Believe Marriage

5. A TIME TO LOVE   97
      The Sexual Conflict
      Life against One Another
      Life for One Another

6. YOUTH IN TRANSITION   121
      Children within the Home
      School, Church, and Neighborhood

7. FROM ONE GENERATION TO ANOTHER   159
      Growing Old in the U.S.A.
      Grandparents in the Home

8. TIME FOR INTIMACY   183
      Dilemmas of Intimacy
      The Promise of Intimacy

LOVE AND CONFLICT

CHAPTER ONE

EMERGENCE OF THE NEW FAMILY

A few years ago, a large industry confronted a young executive with a decision: he could move to a new plant that was being started and get a raise, or he could leave the company. The young executive talked this over with his wife. For a long time he had hoped to get into a business of his own. He had three children and liked the community where he was living. It seemed a shame to leave, just when the children were getting well set in school. Still, he had too little money on hand to start his own business without going way over his head into debt. His wife had a lot of friends in the town whom she would miss. They belonged to the nearby church and were happy about their relationship there. Somehow it did not make sense to move, and yet the company was really giving them no choice.

This is a typical decision of the modern family. Young men and women face problems like this all the time. This young couple took a gamble and went heavily into debt, in order to start a new business and stay in their own community. Thus far, they have made a go of it and are very happy about their decision. But this sets no pattern. It may be wiser for the next man to accept the company's ultimatum, because he may not be able to carry the load of a big debt and establish his own business. There are no clear patterns for decision on these things. Families are pulled apart by the desire to succeed and the need for roots in a community.

In decisions like this, the wife usually represents the home and community ties, while men feel the pull of getting ahead in the company. This is not always true, for there are many women who push their husbands to get ahead at any cost. But, on the whole, women have the bigger stake in the community today, and they are the ones who suffer along with the children from all the moving around. We live in a society that is geared to production, abundance, a rising standard of living, and an expanding economy. These are the watchwords of American life. Someone has to pay the price for this abundance of goods. Today family life is paying the big price. The family has been uprooted. We are like gypsies on the move. We follow the better jobs and the new housing. Our children trail along and change schools. They have friends for a while and then they lose them. Little sense of permanence and security remains. Too often we stand before a decision to keep our roots and fail in our work or succeed in our work and lose our roots.

It is hard to stay in the old neighborhood when one gets a raise. There's more money coming in. We can easily understand the thoughts of a husband concerning a change for his family. . . . "We can have a better car—maybe a Mercury or even a Buick. People on our street don't have Buicks—our street is Fords and Chevies with $14,000 houses. Well, it would be nice to have a Buick, and now we have the money. It would be nice to have a little bigger house too. The kids are getting older and they need a recreation room, so they can invite their friends over without running us out of the living room. It would be hard to leave the gang and the pinochle games at Joe's, but who would dare have a Buick in this block? Everyone would think we were getting stuck up. Oh, hell, let's move and get it over with. The kids will squawk, at first, but they'll have a better school in the

suburb. Look at the school they have to go to now—
forty-five children to a class and double sessions. They'll
make new friends—leave it to them. After all, they'll be
moving around all their lives. They may as well get used
to it now."

And so they move. And so thousands of people from
the southeastern United States stream north every
month. Thousands of people move from one neighborhood of the city to another every week, selling the old
house, financing the new one. No roots! No ties! No real
friends! We are pressed and anxious, but we are doing
better than we did last year, and there is no telling where
we may be next year. "And one thing you can say about
our family, we stick together. We are all we have now—
no roots, no community, no neighborhood, just the family. We can huddle a little closer and keep warm. Nobody knows us in this neighborhood, but at least we
know each other. All this moving has made us a closer
family—too close. We seem to be getting on each other's nerves. If only the children had some friends their
own age. If only they would get out and play. But they
have no real friends now, so we'd better wait and get
to know those people that Joe spoke about—over in the
next block. Well, leave it to the kids—they can get along.
They will make friends."

And then there are the families that stay behind.
They never got that raise. They never could move out.
And they have their thoughts on the subject too. . . .
"Have you noticed how the neighborhood has changed?
You see so many strangers here now, it's not the same
place. Who are all these people anyway and where did
they come from? Did you ever see so many cars parked
on the street? And what a tough element has moved in
across the boulevard. Did you see the mess they made
of that block? Now you have to lock up the bikes at
night and lock the doors. Well, they will never push us

out. We have our house and our church. They can just stay where they belong across the boulevard. We have no use for their kind over here." They were left behind. And they really are a little bitter. They have roots, but the wrong kind! The neighborhood has changed but they will never admit it, so it can never change in a good way. They are living in the past. Something happened to their neighborhood and now they are strangers there.

The family is changing because the world around the family is changing. It is changing faster than any of us would like to admit. The family is not disappearing, as some people thought it would a few years ago. Actually the family has taken a new lease on life. But it is a different family inside and out. A new family is emerging in the midst of all this uprooting and shifting around. A few generations ago, we were country people trying to get used to city life. Even those who had lived for years in cities were really small-town people. But we are becoming big-city people. We are becoming part of that moving flood that sweeps into the city in the morning and flows back out in the evening, like a tide engulfing the metropolis and then receding. Our family is the only secure haven in a world of strangers and uncertainty. "Sure, we know our way around. We can find the place where you get 40 per cent off. We know someone who knows someone who knows a guy who . . . Still, just be sure you check your change. Be sure you watch him put the gas in. Are you sure that he really put a new part in that refrigerator? It's do or be done here! It's kill or be killed! And it's good to get home at night and shut the door on it until tomorrow. It's hard to imagine what those fellows do who don't have families."

A new kind of family is slowly forming under the pressures of this threatening city life. Through newspapers, radio, and TV this new atmosphere is penetrating every village and farmhouse in the country. Industry made the city, and the city is god. The city fashions families to suit its taste—families that can survive in the impersonal, anonymous jungle. Of course, some people are pushing out into suburbia and exurbia, but the city is following them. Each year they have to move further. Now it takes an hour to get to the office—what will it be in ten years, when we are another twenty miles out? Nothing is escaping the urban octopus, least of all the traditional patterns of the American family.

The Pains of Birth

Uncertainty and extremes are keynotes in the birth of a new social pattern. Family life has been going through just such a process. This is a painful and confusing time at the best.

Take, for example, the case of Mary Jones who has two children, aged sixteen and three. When she brought her son home from the hospital sixteen years ago, she had a rigid schedule for his care. He was waked for a feeding if he slept, and permitted to go hungry for an hour or more if he woke at an unscheduled time. He was tied in his crib and handled only when necessary. But Mrs. Jones's baby daughter was in the hospital room with her mother and was fed and cared for whenever mother or child felt the need. Mrs. Jones was astonished at the different techniques of child care recommended by the hospital just thirteen years later. She is troubled also because she has absorbed a certain amount of popular psychology from books and articles written for the new mother. She assumes that the first few years of each child's life will influence his behavior in adolescence and adulthood. Her son at sixteen has many delightful traits. Is her small daughter destined to become quite the opposite because of the different techniques in child care? And, on the other hand, is

Mary Jones directly responsible for her son's unpleasant traits? Mrs. Jones's case is not uncommon today. Many young mothers are quite isolated after marriage these days. They cannot rely on the common sense and experience of a grandmother or aunt, and must find a way through this welter of conflicting advice.

What happened in child care was duplicated in almost every significant aspect of the family's life. The equality of men and women has been an obvious point of uncertainty. If men and women are equal, why should women be stuck in the home? Women receive as much education as men. They have just as much native talent. Why should they waste good minds on carrying out garbage and changing diapers? But somehow getting out into the business world and competing with men also creates problems. What is the best pattern for all concerned? It seems to work out all right for some people and not for others. There have been similar ups and downs in handling adolescents—how much freedom, how much restraint? Questions of premarital sexual experience have disturbed parents and teen-agers. Again and again the question is: what course should we pursue?

This period of extremes and uncertainty has grown out of a changing situation for family life. Such changes in patterns of life do not happen willy-nilly. Industrial work, changing urban neighborhoods, educational needs, rapid transportation, and mass communication have all contributed to this picture. Some parents try to rebel against the changes, reasserting older patterns of domination and control, but these attempts backfire. Somehow it is not that simple. The whole atmosphere of modern life contradicts their views. There is no going back. A new family is emerging. Parents can try to dominate; but schools, radio, movies, and TV are shaping the lives of their children. The problem is not a choice between the old ways and the new. The problem is to discern the necessary and healthy forms in the new.

Development of the New Family

It would be presumptuous to try to list the necessary steps toward the healthy development of the new family, even if it could be done. Many of these steps must be taken without a clear vision. This is, after all, the character of man's responsibility for his own life. Nevertheless, certain forms created in this upheaval of modern life seem to carry promise, while others menace us with deeper separations and uncertainties.

One of the difficulties in the new family is the form in which authority appears. Today authority is like a genie in a bottle. Sometimes we look at our family life and see no authority—just chaos. At other times we sense the pervasive power of a father or more often a mother or, even more often, of the children. Authority is hidden today. It is forced out of sight. We are embarrassed by authority. It is "undemocratic." Democracy has come to mean that everyone is boss. Even the captains of industry talk about "teamwork" and the power elite in politics talks about "the team." One dare not mention power, authority, chain of command, or orders. These words are taboo. We are allergic to authority, but we cannot escape it. So, when our backs are turned, the genie slips out of the bottle.

This is something new in our family life. The old pattern of father's authority has disappeared. The power which mothers always exercised was thus left naked and alone. Mothers used to hold the home together with an authoritative male in the background. And this male figure could afford to stay in the background, because his position was real and unquestioned. Now mothers try to hold the family together on their own. There is no male authority to undergird their discipline.

This rule of mothers may be a temporary development on the route to a new form of democratic authority in the home. That is the most hopeful face to put upon the matter. It is certain that industrial life ended male domination in the family. A man cannot work outside of his home without losing touch with his children. This is not such a misfortune. Male domination is not really a desirable form of authority for the family. And for better or worse, male domination was killed by the commuter's special.

How, then, can any good form come out of the present state of affairs? We are left with several alternatives which may or may not be healthy forms for the new family. We can settle for the rule of mothers. Actually a strong mother with a strong father can make a good parental combination. But a strong mother with no real father figure, except possibly a bumbling Santa Claus who fits in like an old shoe, can make a very one-sided parental combination. It can develop very frustrated and angry boys. It can develop very capable but frigid women. Hence there are some who will not settle for mother rule. What other alternatives are there? We can try the rule of children. This is being experienced in many homes, where parents refuse to take responsibility for ordering their own homes. Or father's authority could be reconstructed in a democratic way. This seems the best alternative, but it needs much more careful interpretation.

One thing is certain. The form in which authority now rears its head in the home is a real problem. We cannot speak hopefully about the emergence of the new family unless we can see a constructive way to fill this vacuum created by the removal of the father from the family setting. All kinds of powers have rushed in to fill this space left by the disappearance of father. Not the least of these powers are the children who are twisting families around their fingers.

Another difficulty in the new family is the loss of perspective on love and marriage. We have fallen "in love with love." The teen-age hysteria over TV idols is no worse than our parental confusion about love. Young couples enter marriage with warm, passionate feelings. Their hearts overflow with possibilities and hope. And in some cases not long after, the young woman is in to tell her story. She was really "in love." She had not been married two months when her husband was out on the town, bored with his wife and seeking excitement. Why? He obviously had no idea of what marriage was all about. She was bewildered. She thought marriage would prolong and deepen the romantic feelings they had had before they married. She never heard of any kind of love except erotic desire. No wonder the girl was bewildered. Romance is a stimulus to marriage, but not its final form. The essence of romance is the inaccessible. Love must take new forms in marriage, if it is to continue. The tragedy of this young woman's marriage, and of so many marriages today, is that couples are disillusioned with love before they discover what it really is.

The romantic view of marriage is hampering the new family in the very process of its birth. Consequently many marriages are stillborn. They never mature. Whether the couple stay together or divorce, they never move beyond the initial disillusionment. We are "in love with love," but we know too little about the full scope of love. We have yet to arrive at a real appreciation of responsible love which finds its fulfillment in life for one another. Many families possess the genuine article but vainly strive to recover the romance from which it emerged. This is a major dilemma confronting the new family.

The family is a total organism. It is similar to a human body. No organ in the body can become diseased without upsetting all parts of the body. An infection in the toe raises the temperature of the body and brings on dizziness and a general feeling of debility. The family is not literally an organism like the body, since it operates by decisions of people and not by automatic responses. Nevertheless, we find in it the same kind of interdependence of parts which we find in the body. Distortion in authority and the struggle to preserve romantic love have disturbed the whole order of family life. We see this disorder in the relations between parents and children, between parents and grandparents. The line of relationships between generations has been disrupted by the changes in the new family.

We all notice how many boys from "good" families and comfortable homes have been caught in vicious crimes in the last ten to twenty years. In each instance the parents have talked about what nice boys they were, how they had never been in trouble. The parents forget to mention that all of this changed with adolescence. The parents are remembering Dick in grammar school. When Dick got to high school, he became grouchy, disobedient, and ultimately delinquent. Why? Why is it that we parents find it so hard to talk to our teen-age children? There are exceptions, but this, in general, is the state of affairs.

Closely related to the teen-age question is the problem of the grandparents. They too are caught up in this breakdown of communication between the generations. Even as the teen-agers are rebelling and pulling up stakes, the grandparents are being retired and shunted off to a corner out of the way. What is back of all this? It is obviously related to all the other disorders in the "organism." This is one problem which seems almost insoluble in our day. There is an Indian tribe in South

America which is purported to have left their old folk to die when they could no longer move to new hunting areas with the tribe. This seems cruel by our standards, and yet it is not nearly as cruel as some of the mental wards and "nursing" homes in which many old folk are being put today. Family life which loses touch with youth and exiles the aged needs reconsidering. A family has to build continuity between old and young, past and future, if it is to prosper in the society and provide the community with healthy citizens. We cannot look at the new form of family life without giving serious consideration to ways in which continuity can grow between the old and the young.

The family is like an organism in its interdependence of parts. It is also like a plant set in a certain soil. The family is not a complete, self-sufficient society. It depends for sustenance upon the larger society in which it grows. This is the soil from which it gains its nurture, so that it, in turn, can serve the larger society. We have already noted that the family has been uprooted. It is a moving, changing, restless thing—never settled long enough to root down into the communal soil of society. Consequently the family has become a plant which can easily perish.

We face two kinds of problems in helping the family put down roots. On the one hand, the family needs contact with neighborhood and community groups, so that it is not merely flotsam in the moving tide of urban life. According to present forecasts, our major cities will see more rather than less population change in the next generation. How can a neighborhood become meaningful with so much coming and going? How can a family take root in a neighborhood of families? On the other hand, there is the larger problem of provision for the very existence of the uprooted family. In times of crisis, families throughout the ages have been helped and supported by relatives and kinfolk. This help may have come in the form of a few bowls of rice or a few bags of corn. Families could always look to relatives to tide them over emergencies. This still happens to some extent. Young couples often make the first payment on the new house with money borrowed from dad and mom. But the situation has changed radically. If the breadwinner gets sick or has a long layoff from work, this can mean disaster to the family today. Most families are living on borrowed capital, deeply in debt for car, house, and furnishings. Very few relatives have the capital to carry the young family through a major crisis. We are in a position in which we need communal support in family crises. We have started in this direction with social security and unemployment compensation. However, other crises still plague the uprooted family. How are we to preserve the integrity and freedom of the family, and yet make provision for its survival as a stable unit?

These are some of the transformations created by industrial and urban life. Each one presents problems to the family. Each one can cripple the family or be molded so as to strengthen and build a healthy family. These are the concerns of this book. How do we detect the creative lines for growth? How do we build the positive trends into a total pattern for the new family?

The Point of View

A few years ago the Russian-dominated government of East Germany attempted to change the marriage laws of that country. This has been a policy of the Russians in satellites which they intend to cripple. They effect a relaxation of the law dealing with the family. Marriage is put on a tentative basis. The stability of the family is shaken and the foundation of the society is undermined. The East German churches struggled against these revisions. After a long period of protest, they were able to check the communists so that family laws would not be revised. The proposed revisions were withdrawn. Nevertheless, the judges began to interpret all cases of family law according to the revisions which had been withdrawn. The communists had retired from the battle, but they had won the day through their control of the judges. Their principal concern was to damage East German character and vitality by undermining family life. They had succeeded in the first round of the battle.

This is an interesting case, because it illustrates the importance attached to a stable family by the communists. A few generations ago, communists in general were talking about the abolition of government and the disappearance of the "bourgeois" family. But Russian experiments with the family in the first few years of the Revolution made it obvious that a society without a strong, stable family life was doomed. The Soviet leaders soon re-established family law and, from that time, used a relaxation in family law only as a means for undermining the character of their satellites.

A society depends upon stable people in order to accomplish its work and execute its political and scientific tasks. People are stable when they grow in an atmosphere of love and order. They have to know what to expect, and they need the reassurance of a responsive concern from others. These are the gifts bestowed upon us by our families, or they are the things which our families have failed to give us. A disordered family cannot produce the stable and responsible people who are so essential to the daily business of a great country. We face this problem of order in our land. A similar problem is overtaking all industrialized countries. A healthy family is not an option for a society. It is a life-and-death matter. We can overlook this crisis for a generation or two. The undermining of the character of a people takes time. Then it begins to accumulate and symptoms of disorder appear on every side. The amount of mental disturbance throughout the society begins to rise rapidly. The reign of lawlessness penetrates to every corner of the society. Vandalism becomes commonplace. Respect for authority in school and family disappears. People begin to crumple under the demands of work. Absentee rolls mount in industry. These are signs of instability. They are not entirely the result of failures in family life. Nevertheless, they cannot be remedied so long as the family is uprooted and disordered.

How, then, are we to decide what is a healthy form in the new family? Who is to say that one direction is more promising than another? This depends upon one's vision of the purpose of the family and how it is intended to serve its members and its society. This depends, in other words, on one's point of view. We need a point of view to make such judgments, just as the communists needed a point of view on the basis of which to decide how to change East German family law. The communists wanted to disrupt the family. Their only question was the best means to gain this objective.

Everyone has a point of view from which he interprets a situation. We see something, and we conclude that it is good, bad, or indifferent. We observe the desegregation of a school system in our community and we feel that it is good or bad, constructive or dangerous. Such an interpretation comes from opinions, beliefs, and ideals which we have received or arrived at in the course of our life experience. Sometimes we hold contradictory beliefs. We may believe in American democracy and still not approve of integrated schools. Nevertheless, each of us has some point of view—some set of values with which we sort out the good and bad aspects of life, however illogical and inconsistent these may seem at times.

The writer's interpretation is built on a biblical conception of family and community life. The Bible is the base of our Judeo-Christian heritage, and it provides a touchstone by which to test new developments in the family. The reader may find himself at odds with this interpretation at times, but, at least, he will know what the writer's point of view is. The reader may also question any particular biblical interpretation, but here again the sources will be given, so that he can make his own judgment. The Bible is not a strait jacket to be pressed down on our changing family. It is not a law book to give "thou shalt's" and "thou shalt not's." The Bible is a witness to God's creative works, to His judgments upon man's disobedience, and above all to His forgiveness and love. The Bible helps us to discern our destiny as persons in community. It sets the changing forms of our communal life in a larger perspective.

This is our vantage point in seeking paths to a healthy life in the family. The reader will have to decide for himself whether or not this vantage point helps him in the uncertainties of a changing society.

CHAPTER TWO

COLD WAR IN THE FAMILY

John is home early from work tonight. He looks again at his watch and muses, "Only 7:15 and Jean still at work getting the four-year-old to bed. Of course, the baby is tucked in, but she'll be awake again at ten. It hardly seems like six years of married life, but there's Susan to remind us that after two years of marriage we had started on family responsibilities. It's funny about Jean. She seems upset a good deal of the time. This is a nice house and a good neighborhood. Changing jobs last year has really paid off, even if they do put more pressure on for week-end work. Why can't Jean relax and enjoy this? Why does she have to gripe about it all the time? If it's not the house, it's the children or the neighbors or the fact that I spend so many Sundays at the office. Of course she does have a dull job, and she stays in with the children too much. Somehow she never seems to get out, though she spends enough time over coffee every morning talking with the girls about how awful their husbands are. This really does Jean a lot of harm, all this griping to the neighbors. Maybe they need more to do. Jean talked about keeping up her writing after Susan came, but she says she never gets time to read, much less to write. It certainly must have been different for our parents. Even her mother finds it hard to understand why she's so upset all the time. She used to be the life of the party, never wanted to go home.

Now, she's tired all the time; and, when she doesn't have a stomach-ache, she's too tired to sit up and see the late movie. Just what has gotten into her anyway?"

This is the way it looks to John, when he gets home and finds the kitchen a mess and no supper on the table. How does it look to Jean? She can't understand it either. . . . One thing is sure, John gives her no support in this job at home. He's gone all day, he sees adults and gets out into the world. Here she is with these little children day in and day out. Why it's months since she's read a book or had a thought. How can you think with tiny children around who exhaust you with diapers and cooking and cleaning? If only people would stop demanding things and just leave her alone. This is such a change from the days when she was studying, discussing ideas, going to concerts and seeing people. Still, she'd hate to be unmarried like Linda, who always tells her how lucky she is. Maybe Linda is right, but it doesn't seem lucky a lot of the time. It would be so nice to be laughing and joking again. John's probably right that she needs to get out more, but how can she get out? Who's going to take the baby? Susan is no trouble, but the baby is just too much. Mother's been good about helping out, but she's so exhausted after an afternoon with the baby that it hardly seems fair to ask her. And then mother is always making remarks about how the children are not warmly dressed and they need more discipline. It's hard enough to do this job without a lot of criticism. . . .

Nobody really seems at fault in this house. Both John and Jean do their jobs pretty well. The children are being raised, even if it is not to grandmother's liking. Why, then, do they both feel so unsettled about their home and discontented with the way things are going? Why does Jean find it so hard to settle down and do her work without complaints and stomach-aches? Why does John feel so uncertain about his place in his own home and what he should do to help? One minute he is tempted to take over the kitchen and do what Jean has left undone. Another minute he feels like giving Jean a swift kick. Jean seems to be too much in the house. John seems to be too much outside the orbit of his family's life. This couple, who were so much in love a few years ago, have now begun to drift apart. Each one resents the other, and yet neither knows what he or she resents. Jean would like to be a wife, but she feels so stuck being a mother that she's forgotten how to be a wife. John would like to be a father in the family, but he is so baffled by the whole situation that he does not know where to begin. This is cold war in the family. Neither partner in the marriage remembers how or why it started. Neither one knows what to do in order to end it.

Many steps need to be taken to break down the curtain of confusion which has led to the cold war. One step is dealing with the place of the father in the family. In fact, one aspect of the problem is that he has little or no place in the family. This is not the only reason or even the most important one for the cold war, but nothing can be done until John re-enters his home as "somebody."

Father's Abdication

The first thing that John has to face is the fact that his work has removed him from the family's orbit. He plays in a different league. John's influence as father in his home has been annihilated by modern work in office and factory. A few centuries ago it was unusual for a man to have his work away from his home. If he ran a store, he lived over or behind it. If he made things or fixed things, he did it around his house. Merchants, seafaring people, and soldiers were a minority whose work was divorced from the family. Ordinary mortals worked near or in their homes.

The change in place of work from home to factory has upset the authority picture in the family. It has changed father's relation to the family. James Thurber touched on this in one of his essays. He described his maid's confusion over the fact that he always seemed to be around the home. She had relatives who worked *into* offices and factories, and she was perplexed to see Thurber constantly about the house. A man just ought to be out of the house. Father is the mysterious figure who spends his time out of the house.

This change in setting for work has been developing for a century. Only in the last generation, however, has long-range commuting by car and train become commonplace. "The Man in the Gray Flannel Suit" on the commuters' special is now a common type—not a banker, just a suburbanite. His work and his family are two separate worlds, and they seldom meet. A suburban pastor was calling on his men at their work not long ago. He had occasion from time to time to check their work addresses with their wives before calling. To his amazement, many wives did not know the location of their husbands' jobs. They knew the line of work, but they had little notion of where it was carried on.

Father has become a stranger in his own home. He arrives home for a late supper and sees his children as they are about to go to bed. He has little contact with these children. They have little or no idea what he does. He may be gruff or friendly, sad or joyful, loved or tolerated, but he is more guest than parent, more visitor than member. Walt Disney's movie on Eskimo culture gave us an idea of "who" father used to be. He was a very important "somebody." Boys learned every skill from him—skills which meant life or death. That is Eskimo life today. It was, in a sense, American life a century ago. Industrial development changed all that. Children learn their skills in school and, later, on the job. Father may be dearly loved and often is; but, as a power in the home, he is nobody. Father has abdicated, or rather his work has forced him out of his place in the home.

Of course, family survival depends on the work which father does. He knows this and his wife usually realizes it. But it is hard for the children to see and understand this. Mother buys the food. She prepares the meals and picks out the clothes and furniture. She seems to be the source of all the good things which they have. Father's contribution is a pay check which children cannot understand or interpret. However important he may be to the family in fact, he simply does not seem important to the children. The world of work, where he may be very important, is an unknown world to them. Many families never know father's real prestige until his funeral. Then they are often amazed to discover that he had a complete world in which they never shared.

The fact that a father's principal relationship to his home is through money—a pay check at that—makes it extremely difficult for his children to understand what he is doing for them. We adults are used to dealing with money, and we forget that money is a very technical means of exchange. Simpler societies have used wampum and other symbols for exchange, but money is a very abstract symbol. The actual paper in a dollar bill is, of course, worthless. We see this when small children get hold of paper money and readily trade it for a penny. As children get older they can begin to understand what a father does for a family in bringing home a pay check, but they will remain confused as to how he earns this money. If money is an abstract symbol, modern industrial and office work is even more difficult to understand. Modern industrial plants fill reams of paper with job descriptions for different operations. Each job is classified and described in detail. The operations on a particular job may be quite simple, but it takes an engineer to know what those few operations are really accomplishing in the total process of production. A man's wife and children can hardly be expected to understand his job. Wife and children are alienated from the orbit of the father's life. It is remarkable how many times one asks a man about his work in front of his family, and the first comments of surprise come from the family as they hear what he does.

Money and technological work in a place removed from the home have made father a stranger in his home. It is no wonder John feels uncertain about the situation at home. It is hard to know where to step in, what to do, what course to take. He is too much out of the family's orbit to know where to start. The family is too removed from his world to be of much help in drawing him into a real place in the home.

Mother Is "All"

As father's work has taken him further and further from home, mother has become more and more the center of the family. This is a familiar story. Everyone has heard of "mom" and all her works. Few people seem to realize that she was left with this family and had little choice about becoming "mom."

We have come to a strange state of affairs. The world of work is a man's world in which a few very energetic women can hew out a small foothold. But the family world is a woman's world, where "mom" rules and dad visits. Mom has to work out her life on the home front. Dad has to alternate between two entirely different worlds—home and job. However big or little he is on the job, at home he has to fit into a going concern as a minor shareholder.

Our comic strips are quite a commentary on this home situation. In such varied strips as Blondie, Li'l Abner, Dottie Dripple, and even Joe Palooka, the men are portrayed as stupid though fairly genial. The women are consistently the managers and centers of power. Mammy Yokum is not a bad caricature of the American mom and Joe Palooka's mother is the epitome of the true mom herself.

This is the authority setup in the new family. There are obviously many exceptions and all kinds of variations. But this is a major outline of how things are working out. At the moment, father has lost his power to direct his children. He is not even a leader among equals. He can come home and try to sound important, but he carries little weight in the situation. He may have a lot to say about the new car or the vacation trip, but he has lost touch with the children's discipline. This, in itself, might not be much of a problem, but it is making him lose touch with his wife. Her life is lived in the home with the children. If he loses touch with this, he loses touch with her. She then finds herself in the strange position of having to give her attention either to her husband or to her children. She is no longer sharing jointly in a life with her husband which includes her children.

The Mixed Feelings of a Woman

Women are in a peculiar situation in America. Outside the home they are really second-class citizens. It *is* a man's world on the outside. This would not be quite so hard to accept if the women were uneducated and fit only for housework. Actually they are as well educated as men—and quite as capable. Most women have the feeling that they are wasting their education and talents

on housework. This does not make it any easier for
women to build up their husbands' importance in the
home. They cannot help resenting the fact that the men
spend so much of their time outside in "that exciting
world." Women can very easily take out their resentment
over being second-class citizens by refusing to build up
their husbands' significance in the family. On the other
hand, a woman who loves her husband cannot help
wishing that he could be a strong and important person
around the house. Most women really want a husband
who is "somebody." It is not enough for him to be important at his work or to be doing a significant job at
the plant. If the wife has to live her life in the home,
she would like to have a strong husband and father in
the home.

Many women have very mixed feelings about this new
power situation. They are saddled with the whole direction of the family. They cannot help but feel, at
times, that they are second-class citizens in the outside
world. It helps a little to be boss at least in the family.
And yet it would be a big help to have a husband who
could take some responsibility about Johnny's trouble
in school and Jane's late hours. At this point there is a
deadlock in most homes on the power question. This is
cold war.

One alternative to mother's rule is to surrender power
to the children. Some women have retreated from the
spotlight, and the children have taken control. A Japanese clergyman, who studied for three years in one of
our seminaries, was much troubled by this rule of the
children during his pastoral visits. He pointed out to the
rector of the parish that he was accustomed in Japan to
addressing the father of the house. It had soon become
evident to him that the father in America was not a
significant person in the family, so he began addressing

his remarks to the mother. He soon found that he had to deal with the children, since they seemed to be the dominant figures in the family.

Child rule is the inevitable result of the father's abdication. It is a natural development in America. We Americans idolize children and youth. Most of us feel that our children should have the best of everything. It is very easy for the American family to gear all its plans to transporting the children, picking up after them, and listening to their endless chatter or silencing the guests so that they can see their favorite TV show. This is the last stage of the cold war. Women refuse to be the center of family life. If father has abdicated and mother withdraws, then the children will rule.

There is a good and bad side to the developing power of children in the family. The good side is clearly the opening of the way to more expressiveness and personal creativity for children. This, at least, is the assumption of the new view of rearing children. Children are not animals to be fed and herded about. They are not grownups who still happen to be small in size by some quirk of nature. They are children in the process of becoming adults. They are persons with the feelings and needs of any human being. They need to speak and receive responses. They may stumble and falter in telling a story, but they need an opportunity to express themselves in a warm and understanding atmosphere. This is the good side of the new place of children in the family.

The unfortunate side of this developing power of children is the unhappy effect of disorder upon them. Children need order and stability, in order to develop their best capacities. There is always a tension between order and freedom. Children need freedom to try their wings. They also need enough order to work away at this business of growing up within boundaries which protect their lives and give them sound assurance of what they can expect. We have all seen the unhappy effects of removing all restraints from children and young people. Many young people never adjust to the demands of work, because no one cared enough about them to discipline them. Imposing order in a home is a form of love, since it expresses the concern and affection of the parents for the growth of the children. It is easier to be tyrannical, on the one hand; or to let the children run riot, on the other. Tyranny and license are unloving ways of dealing with children, because they are ways of satisfying the needs of the parents rather than the needs of the children. Love really cannot be separated from discipline, which is part of what the Bible means when it says, "Whom the Lord loveth He chasteneth." The license that leads to the rule of children is an unloving way of exercising parental responsibility.

It is difficult to maintain a middle way between tyranny and license. It is much easier to flop over on one side or the other. Our ancestors tended to take the side of tyranny, since this fitted the whole atmosphere of their day. We tend to take the side of license, since this fulfills certain needs peculiar to our own time. We tend to live in the future today, and it is easy to identify the future with the children. We are always working for something which we can buy, earn, win, or achieve. This attitude is reflected in the emphasis on youth in our time. Children are a symbol of the new that is yet to be fulfilled. Youth is the symbol of the new and untried. The present may be a bit shabby, but it will soon be different. Our children will have privileges which we missed—the future must be served and it will be served by bowing down to youth.

Furthermore, we resist authority and discipline in our day. This may come from the impersonal forms of authority in our work—piece rates of production are enforced by a machine which engineers have set, and we have to look for credit to companies who treat us as accounts rather than persons. Certainly, this is part of it. It may also come from rebellion against the rule of the mothers, which is ultimately a rule of home and heart rather than business and community. But, whatever the sources, the resistance to authority is deep within us and it encourages us to think that we are loving our children by letting them do as they wish. And, finally, popular psychology has stressed the dangerous effects of repression on children. This has led to confusion between orderly restraint and repression. Everyone needs the restraints of discipline, law, and order, because everyone has tendencies to make the world his oyster and all men his slaves. It is human to submit to explicit commands of morality and decency. The repressive forces that hurt us and disturb us are those experiences which call into question our whole right to exist. This can be illustrated by the difference between criticism and sarcasm. Criticism helps us see where we have erred and why. It assumes that we are capable of doing differently in this specific operation, and it is given only with regard to that in which we have erred. Criticism should leave us intact as persons. Sarcasm, on the other hand, is an attack on the person as such through an attack on a defect or error in the person. Sarcasm brings into question the person's right to be; and, coming from a significant person like a parent, can annihilate any sense of confidence or self-assurance. Popular psychology has led many parents to fear discipline, when the real insight of psychology points to the need for order and the danger of personal rejection.

It is in this atmosphere that the rule of the children has developed. It is reflected in subtle ways. Our families tend to be preoccupied with children to the point of eliminating any significant personal life for the adults. We tend to live out our desires for freedom through the license we give to the children. Nothing is too good for the children, so it becomes more and more difficult for them to see the point of hard and careful work. "Things have come easily" is soon translated into "Things should come easily." Thus we come to the child-centered family which is ruled by tyrannical children who are insatiable in their demands for service. This not only destroys any framework in which children can mature, but also sets the children at war with one another. In the daily life of the family, this is probably the most disturbing sympton of the rule of the children. Once the framework of orderly parental rule is taken away, the children begin to compete for domination. This is like civil war, since not all can rule and each must compete for control. This internal warfare in the modern family has led many parents to begin a more disciplined management of their homes, for they have seen that license in the home ultimately destroys any community in the family. The rule of children is more common today than is generally admitted. It causes parents to resent their children. It is like the host who lets his guests impose and then resents the guests for imposing. Parents suddenly wake up to find that they are waiting on their children hand and foot. This is a miserable discovery to make. They cannot help resenting their children, even though it is their own fault.

Why Mother Can't Be "All"

Women are in a difficult position in the modern family. To be sure, they have their resentments and mixed feelings—some of them get a little dizzy with power. But there are fundamental reasons why mother can't be "all." In the true Amish meaning of "all," to be dead, the mother who takes over the whole family will be killed in the crossfire, and deep down she knows it. A look at the real nature of parental authority reveals the ambiguity of woman's position in the home today.

Anyone who exercises leadership can expect to be disliked. This is the price one pays to be a leader.* Most of us have experienced this in groups, committees and organizations. Most of us want to be liked, so it is hard to pay this price for leadership. An essential quality of a leader is a willingness to take criticism. This is not said cynically. In America, at least, no one likes to be led. We see this very clearly in many of the studies which have been made of committees and groups in which persons exercise leadership. The man with the best ideas and suggestions is exercising real leadership. It soon develops that the man with the best ideas is not very well liked. He may be respected for his ideas; the group may even follow his suggestions; but he will not be liked. This is part of the cost of being a leader.

We get another insight into leadership from the study of groups. Groups need a leader with good ideas who will make suggestions, but they also need a member who is well liked and who can keep everyone together. We have all seen such people in groups. They pat people on the back, encourage them to get in a word, and generally help knit people together. These are the people who hold a group together while it goes about the job of solving its problems. These members are usually the best-liked people in the group. A strong and effective group develops when this best-liked person allies himself with the leader who is making the suggestions. If the best-liked person will support the leader, the group can move ahead and work out its problems. Without such an alliance, however, the leader can easily become so isolated by the resentment of the group that he loses

* The author is indebted to the work of R. F. Bales for the insights in the treatment of leadership.

his power. If this happens, the leadership dwindles and the group ends up bickering.

The mother should really fill this role of best-liked person in the family. She should become the member who supports the weak, encourages the crestfallen, and holds the family together as a group. This, at least, seems to be the proper fulfillment of her feminine role. As she lends support to her husband's leadership, the family is knit together and can solve its problems.

Of course, a mother is both leader and supporter of her infant child. In the first years of a child's life, the mother is trying to lead the child gently toward responsibility and more mature membership in the family. She also nurtures and supports the child. The mother usually has to carry the brunt of the leadership through these early years and depends on the support and backing of the older members of the family. She is always trying to keep the child from slipping back into thumb sucking or bed wetting, but at the same time she is encouraging and even indulging the child. As each child comes along, mother has some years in which she is both leader and best-liked person.

As the children reach five or six years of age, they have to meet demands from outside the home. They have to adjust to school and neighborhood. This is the time when mother should be moving into the position of best-liked person who is supporting and encouraging. She should be moving from bottom-slapping to back slapping. Mothers inevitably have poorer perspective on these outside demands, since the main focus of their lives is in the home. It is the father who lives the major part of his life outside and can most adequately represent these outside demands to the children. When mothers have to represent these expectations, they usually end up nagging and distorting them. It is a rare mother who can escape seeing her growing children a objects to be protected. It is not possible or constructive for a mother to continue in this double position as leader and best-liked when her children begin to mature and meet expectations outside the home. This is too mixed a role for a mother to fulfill.

But it is not easy for father to step into the leadership role when he is so removed from the family and has had so little part in the family life up to this time. It would seem the most natural thing in the world for fathers to move into this position of leadership as their children begin to face the adjustment to school and friends. In some cases, obviously, they do. Most often, however, there are two things which prevent this natural development of a father's leadership. First, he has had almost no power in the family up to this time. Habits are hard to change. The children just do not see him as a significant leader of their activities. Second, most fathers are under a lot of competitive pressure in their jobs. They may compete with other workers or machines. In either case, the world of work drains their feelings of adequacy and personal assurance. This business of manipulating other people or being manipulated by them does not build up one's personal life. It drains and exhausts. Few men come home from such work willing to accept the resentment of the children against their leadership. Too often the fathers are looking for support and personal reassurance at home. They come home looking for encouragement rather than responsibility. As parents, men tend to take to the best-liked role in the home. They may bring presents, they may give gum or money; whereas mother is more demanding in her gifts, since she is trying to build responsibility in the children. The pressures of work lead fathers toward the line of least resistance in dealing with their children. For these reasons, men do not fall naturally into leadership as it is needed in the home. So mother too often finds herself in the crossfire. She cannot be "all" but she has to be "all." She should be in the role of best-liked, but she ends up as leader.

The Escape from the Home

This picture of the family mixup seems a little overdone when it is spelled out this way. Our inclination is to say that this must be some other family—not ours. But there are symptoms of this inner disorder which we cannot escape.

One symptom of disorder is the fact that many women today find housework and home life depressing and unsatisfying. Of course there are many reasons for this. Much of housework *is* routine and even dull. It is a constant picking up and cleaning up of the same old things. And the home is more a place to wait for the family car than a center of important activities. But all this does not explain the deep frustration of women today—their desire to escape into something outside. What is outside? There is hard, monotonous work outside. There is exhausting running from one committee to another on the outside. There is the difficult task of holding a job and rushing home to be the homemaker on Saturday and Sunday. Many women have taken on a full job outside in addition to their housework. Why? Sometimes for money, to be sure. But just as often to escape the ambiguous task of being both leader and supporting person in the family!

Another symptom is the perplexed look on father's face as he sees the home situation. He wants nothing more than to sit and enjoy the quiet, friendly atmosphere of his home. It all seems so simple. He has earned enough for a home, so that his family can be comfortable and happy. What is there to get so excited about? Why all this push to get out—to go somewhere, do something? What could be nicer than this home, these children, the TV program, and the house to fix? Then there is the week-end for a little golf, some fishing, work in the yard, or a little "do-it-yourself" repair. But his wife says she is so busy being a mother that she cannot be a wife. She feels all mixed up between this business of directing her children and giving affection to her husband. She has endless accounts of frustrations with children and neighbors. She cannot seem to see that people never had such an easy and comfortable situation.

And then we have the children. As they grow into their teens, they seem so unruly. They do not listen to their mother. Father occasionally speaks harshly and lays down the law, but it does not seem to do much good. They were such good children before, but now they seem distant and preoccupied. They help around the house only when they are pushed into it. One would think that this was not even their home. Somehow it just is not working out the way it should. A family should be a happy, friendly group, but the children always seem to be squabbling and teasing one another. Mother wants to get out. Dad wants to relax and stay at home. The children seem to live their real lives somewhere else.

No family feels all these strains and tensions at any particular moment. Families have their high days and their low days, and they also have the days which just seem to go by. Somehow the days pass and the children grow and things seem to work out one way or another. The strains created by the abdication of father and the ambiguous role of mother are usually felt only as a sense of uneasiness in the family. These tensions are felt in the family as a kind of disquiet and uncertainty. The cold war is mostly beneath the surface.

In the midst of all this, there is the sense that the family could be something more than this. There is the hope that family life could develop in a freer and more creative way. This is not a false hope. It is not an unreasonable feeling of disquiet. Many of these problems can be resolved through a proper perspective and a clearer course of action. The present situation is creating an undue amount of anxiety throughout all of American life. It is possible and necessary that we work out sound leadership in this new kind of family.

The life of a family is a whole. Leadership is only one part of the whole. Other facets of the disorder need to be considered along with leadership. These additional aspects will be considered in succeeding chapters. It is particularly important to remember, as we consider a possible solution to the problem of leadership, that this alone cannot bring order and love. It is, nevertheless, a fundamental source of difficulty for the new family.

CHAPTER THREE

FATHER IN FACT

We face a peculiar problem in dealing with the confusion of leadership in our homes. Though we can see each day that father is no longer the actual leader, we still think of him as head of the family. As long as we keep on thinking that he is the actual authority, little can be done. Until we recognize that we have a problem, we cannot deal with it. For instance, one of the most difficult aspects of alcoholism is that most alcoholics refuse to face the fact that drink has the better of them. Until they admit this, no one can really help them. When they "hit bottom" and face facts, friends can begin to help. And when the alcoholic faces his situation, he is well on the way to solving his problem.

The preceding chapter attempted to make clear some of our modern confusion about parental authority. We naturally react to this by saying that it does not apply to us. However, a solution to this problem is only possible if we face the situation, and then decide to do something about it. Facing this situation means that we really want to restore father to the family. We must want him to be the leader of the home in fact as well as fancy.

But is there any good reason to think that we ought to reverse history and re-establish the father in the home? Is this perhaps a nostalgia for the past to which we can say good riddance? Is there any sound reason for claiming that a significant father is *essential* for the healthy development of his family? We have considered signs of disorder and confusion, but there are other explanations for these. Just what is the basis for claiming that the father should be the head of the family?

Male and Female

It used to be common to talk about a "natural" superiority of men. The general line was that men should lead in home and community because they were bigger, wiser, more capable, etc., etc. This whole idea has been attacked by feminists and those who have studied other societies. In fact, the pendulum has swung so far the other way that Ashley Montagu recently wrote a book on *The Natural Superiority of Women.* So it is very difficult to base an argument for father's leadership in the home on a "natural superiority." Such an argument cuts both ways and could as well be used in favor of women.

Nevertheless, there are two facts about men in our society which make one feel that it is essential for them to lead in the home. We have already touched on one fact—the role of men in the larger community of industrial and agricultural production. For better or worse, men are the chief workers outside the home setting. They till the fields, tend the machines, plan the computers, sell the merchandise, and truck the goods. Of course many mothers work outside the home today. However, a mother rarely invests her deepest concerns and ambitions in her occupation outside the home. She is almost always rooted primarily in her concern for the children. The argument here, then, is quite clear: if children are to be guided into responsible participation outside the home in school and work, that guidance should come from the parent whose life is rooted in the world of work outside the home. Both husband and wife have concerns inside and outside the family. The one who leads does not exclude the other; that would not be leadership but domination. This is not a question of exclusive but of shared responsibility in which one must take the lead. There is no question that the chief wage-earner is rooted in the world outside the home and can most adequately represent those demands in the home.

But this division of responsibility inside and outside the home is not simply an accident. There is a natural basis for it in the physiological and temperamental differences between men and women. This is not "natural superiority." It is a difference in function through which men and women complement one another. We have to look behind our gadgets and machines to the flesh-and-blood men and women to see this. Only a very starry-eyed feminist would claim that male and female temperaments are the same. A feminist might claim that woman's job of taking care of children has given her this temperament, but this leads to the unanswerable chicken-and-egg argument—who is to say which came first? Being a woman and bearing children leads to child care which softens a temperament and disposes a person to care for the home. What came first here? Does that really matter? The real point is that there is a physiological basis for a difference of temperament which no one can think out of existence.

The real physiological difference is reflected in the distinctive roles in sexual intercourse. The male must prove his masculinity or there will be no intercourse. A woman can be fulfilled in the relationship only to the extent that this is demonstrated. Her role, on the other hand, is to accept and receive. In this physiological difference of function can be seen the whole pattern of difference in leadership. Obviously this is not a question of which is better—superior or inferior. It is simply a matter of who is to take the aggressive, leading role.

In the sexual relationship, the aggressive and leading pattern is clearly a male role.

The leading role of men is reinforced as women enter upon childbearing. In fulfilling her sexual role by receiving her husband, she becomes even more dependent upon him in bearing his child. There is, of course, a mutual dependence in marriage or it would not be a relationship. But after childbirth a wife depends on her husband for her own survival and the life of her child. Now she is limited in her freedom to work or travel, because she is burdened with the feeding and care of her infant. Of course, bottle feeding and nurses may free her to a large extent, but in the order of nature she is bound by breast-feeding and the infant's need for the affection of the feeder. A mother's holding and handling of her infant are *just as important* to growth as the food she provides. Thus, the woman increases her dependence on the man in her own demonstration of her womanhood. She thrusts him further into the responsibilities of leadership.

The fulfillment of sexual intercourse in childbirth puts the man even more in the aggressive position. He must, if he is a responsible person, demonstrate even further his masculine capacity to provide for his wife and child. They are dependent on him, and he must protect them as well as provide for them. This, in the order of human life, is a "natural" division of responsibilities. It does not hold in the animal world, for the most part, because few animals have the problem of long dependency of the young on the nurture of the parents. Most animal young can forage for food with the mother not long after birth. We are not considering a natural order of all creation, but rather the human order of life in its natural forms.

Human beings have manipulated this protective male role in various ways. Man is always altering natural proc esses through his intellectual powers. It is true that there are societies in which women have carried both the food-gathering and the child care. One or the other usually suffers in the process. It is also true that husbands in some societies have had little responsibility for their family. But in these cases the uncle takes the responsibility. A man, husband or relative, usually has significant responsibility for the welfare and leadership of the family. All these variations suggest that we are dealing with a flexible order which human society can modify for good or ill. We live in a society in which a husband is responsible for his own family rather than his sister's. The chief point still holds—man is responsible for leadership. He represents the family in the world outside the family and he comes into the family as protector and as representative of these demands.

Husband and Wife in the Bible

It is in this vein that we can understand the, to modern ears, rather strange New Testament comparison of husband and wife to Christ and His Church. Since the overall frame of reference of this book has been said to be the biblical point of view, a note is appended to this chapter on husband and wife in the Bible (see p. 65), but some treatment of this belongs in the text here.

The father, in the Israelite family in the Old Testament, held the dominating position and was actually viewed as a source of strength for the whole family and all the blood children. He was, in a sense, possessor not only of his domestic animals and property but also of his wife. Even though women had protection of their status and rights, the figure of the male had predominance with both a social and religious sanction.

The new element introduced into the marriage relationship in the New Testament is a new status for the wife, epitomized in a sentence in one of Paul's letters (Ephesians 5:21): "Be subject to one another out of reverence for Christ." The husband continues as answerable to God for the order and welfare of his family, but the family is no longer his possession to use and enjoy; the family is a place where his ministry of love is to be expressed.

A New Alliance of Husband and Wife

Modern life has finally broken the arbitrary domination of men and freed women for a responsible role in society. Mutuality of love and responsibility is a practical possibility in the modern family. At present, however, we are seeking this freedom by throwing out all authority and subordination in the alliance. We are in no danger of restoring an arbitrary male domination. Our problem is quite the reverse. We are in danger of losing any male quality in our home life, with disastrous consequences for the whole family.

Even those parents who are aware of this feel that it is hopeless. How can a man take a leading place within his home when he is so seldom there and so preoccupied with his work day and night? Even if we grant that God intends us to have a marriage of mutual love in which the husband-father is to lead—a democratic marriage with male leadership—how can this come about in the modern home?

One essential step in the restoration of fatherhood is the introduction of fathers into the responsibility for discipline of children. There was no need for this a few generations ago. The wife in an early-American family could easily handle all the discipline up to the time of adolescence. There was never any question about the father's position in the family. She could turn over responsibility to him at any time and his position was such that he could carry it. If the wife carries all the discipline for the children up to adolescence today, she finds that there is no father to whom the responsibility can be transferred as the children get older. If father is not introduced into the situation earlier than the time of the children's adolescence, he will have abdicated long since. For better or worse, it looks as though the men will have to get in on the discipline by the time the children reach the age of three or four. Let us consider concretely what this would mean and how difficult it would be.

Father returns at suppertime. He arrives when mother is tired and the children are inclined to be hungry and grouchy. He has not been in on the family events of the day. He, too, is tired and would like to relax before supper. But five-year-old Susie has been tormenting her three-year-old brother for an hour, and by now the brother is quite unbearable. Father's natural tendency would be either to hide from this confusion behind his newspaper and let his wife handle it, or else to discipline unjustly the young brother. If he is to enter creatively into the authoritative position, he must ask for his wife's interpretation of the situation and act accordingly. He must also have her support as the best-liked member. Provided he is informed, a father is really in a much better position to dispense justice at this point in the day than the mother. By six o'clock mother is usually so wrought up over the situation, having dealt with it all through the day, that she finds it difficult to dispense justice with any kind of objectivity. There are two important points involved here. First, if the father is to participate in the discipline of the children, he needs the guidance and support of his wife. Second, although it would be much easier for the man to escape this confusion, he really has a great deal to contribute to the whole family by sharing in it.

This is not suggesting that we return to the old days of mother's threat, "Just wait until your father comes home and he'll take care of you." A mother has to discipline when a situation arises. She too participates in the coalition which has responsibility for the children. She too is a parent. The only issue is whether father assumes his responsibilities when he gets home.

It is very difficult for most men to get involved in this home situation after a hard day at work. They have a great many things on their minds, and they are tired from the hard, competitive struggle of their work. Many of them commute for hours on crowded trains or highways. It is not easy to come into a home and have to take additional responsibility for the ordering of the lives of the children. Many men just throw up their hands at this possibility and refuse to have anything to do with it, and one cannot help but sympathize with them. The fact is, however, that their children need to have them take this kind of responsibility. Their children need a father who stands for something in the home. Women need a husband who will support their work in the home by being a real person when he is on the premises. He simply cannot be a real person as long as the children are controlling the household. Many men have sensed the need for this kind of earlier participation in the discipline of the children, and one finds them today attending at childbirth and giving real attention in the evenings to the care and feeding of the children. All this represents a sign that men sense the importance of becoming more involved with their children. Obviously men should not usurp the mother's role of care and nurture. But children must experience a father's direction at an earlier age if they are to accept his authority in later years.

It is foolish to think that this is an easy thing to do in our day and age. It all comes down to a father's taking serious responsibility within his own home, as well as in his job, which means that he has a double focus for his life. It also comes down to the woman's interpreting her discipline of the children so that they realize that she is exercising an authority in alliance with her husband. Men are so pressed by their work and pour out their lives so completely in their occupations that this shift to the focus in the home is difficult. Nevertheless, when men and women see that this would contribute immeasurably to the stability of their homes, many of them are willing to try it.

Introducing men to a real share in child discipline is only a first step in the restoration of fatherhood to the home. There are many other ways in which they will have to take responsibility for the family if they are to have a significant share in the development and growth of their children. There is a growing tendency today for the wife to handle the family money. This is convenient and natural because of the importance of household buying. Many families are so deeply in debt that the only money which is not already allocated is the money which goes into the household. Nevertheless, children do receive allowances from their parents and they also receive money for special things. This is the kind of thing which a woman should place very carefully in the hands of the father. There is no way that children, particularly when they are small, can understand that the father is really earning the income of the family. A check means nothing to a small child. They need to sense and see things which indicate that the money which they spend for their candy and movies has some relationship to their fathers. This is the beginning of a child's understanding of the extent to which his welfare depends on his father as well as his mother. This is not taking anything away from the mother's share of the child's dependency period. The trouble with most of our children these days is that they are too dependent on their mothers. This is the kind of thing which can help to restore a father to some place within the home.

The purpose of all this is not to make a fetish of the father. And it is not a question of turning the man into a new kind of mother. The point is that the wife needs a husband in the home who is a real man and has a real place. Furthermore, the children need a man in the home who is a real father and a real person. He can only be this if he is somebody in the home. He can only be somebody in the home if he says and does things which are important in their lives. By the time they reach adolescence, they can have a real relationship with a father who has had something to do with their lives as they have been maturing. If the father has carried his responsibility through these years, the mother can very easily move into the role of best-liked guide and supporter for the emotional and personal lives of the members of the family. She can lend her support to her husband's leadership. The father can complement her role in relationship to the children by carrying the responsibility of seeing that they fulfill the demands imposed upon them by school and job and community. This is the result of a complete change of attitude in the earlier years by both the father and the mother. It is not merely a matter of a few gimmicks or a few disciplinary tricks. The man and the woman have to begin to think of themselves as male and female, trying to fulfill the responsibilities given to them by their own destiny in the family. This is not a gimmick. It is a new life. It is a new alliance. It is a new kind of father and mother appropriate to the new family.

We can recall here what was said about groups in which the best-liked member, who holds the group together, withdraws his support from the leader with the best ideas. Without this support, the leader is isolated by resentment in the group. His leadership collapses. The group ends up bickering and accomplishes very little. This alliance between leader and best-liked is crucial for the successful operation of a group. It is equally essential in a family. A father cannot successfully lead his family if his wife sabotages his leadership. This has to be a real coalition with mutual understanding and confidence. The children have to feel the influence of the mother guiding them toward conformity with their father's demands. This is the real meaning of an alliance between father and mother—a coalition of power to which each brings different gifts. The alliance will fail if the husband refuses to give creative and sensitive attention to the needs of his family. It will also fail if the wife takes a neutral, "wait-and-see" attitude toward her husband's leadership. This has to be a coalition of powers in the fullest sense. The development of this coalition in a democratic form is a small but essential step toward a healthy family life.

Woman's Position in the New Family

The restoration of men to leadership in the home is only one part of the reordering of family life. Much was said in the preceding chapter about the tensions created by the position of the modern housewife. She is isolated from her relatives. She is often living in a neighborhood amid strangers. She has very often received a good education and has many talents which she cannot express in her home. She is free, but she is bound to the house and spends most of her time with people who are under the age of six. However much joy she may find in her children, she soon feels that her mind is stagnating and that she too is less than six. Her great-grandmother's housework entailed a lot of creative work, but she finds that her housework is utterly simple and most of it extremely dull. It is not enough for men to find their way back into a significant place in the home. Women, too, must find expression for their lives if the family is to achieve some balance in its inner life.

Some women do not feel that this is a problem, and for them obviously it is not. There are many differences of personality and circumstance which make it hard to generalize about this dilemma of the modern woman. There is clearly no simple solution. There are many other women who are very conscious of this problem and would like to work out a creative solution. Actually the majority of women are not satisfied with their job in the home and do not feel that it really uses their capacities. It would be a mistake to think that the authority problem in their homes will be resolved by restoring the man to his true position. They will still find themselves chafing at the bit and sabotaging their husbands' leadership. It is only realistic to look for some creative use for the talents of such women.

Some women have solved this problem by taking a part-time job or even working full time. This is difficult, when the children are small, although some women have been able to do it. It is obvious that these women are working because they feel a need for a creative outlet, since they very rarely earn more than enough money to pay for the help which has to be hired to meet housekeeping responsibilities. Nevertheless, this has worked out as a satisfactory solution for a good many women. It is certainly one possibility, and congenial to women who have a particular interest or a particular training. Most couples who have a reasonable relationship with one another can get along with this situation, provided the wife is not a lot more successful than the husband. If real economic competition between husband and wife begins to arise in a situation like this, it can be very dangerous to the security of the marriage.

This again depends a great deal on the security and stability of both members in the marriage.

The group of women who seem to have the most difficulty in finding an adequate outlet for their abilities in the form of a job are those whose talents are artistic. There are, of course, some women who startle their friends by raising large families and doing all sorts of artistic and creative work. They are, however, the exception. An artist's work is rarely paid enough to make it possible for women to get other people to do their housework while they take time for creative work. Consequently they find themselves struggling to do it at home while carrying the full load of housework and the care of children. This can be a most difficult and frustrating experience.

There are other outlets which many women have used to express themselves. Much of the work that is being done in churches, volunteer organizations, and political associations by women is an expression of some of this creative energy which is bottled up in the homes. A lot of this is useful and creative work for which the larger community can be very grateful. Nevertheless, much of this work is unsatisfying for the women who do it and reduces itself to a rather impersonal kind of committee operation. It is unfortunate that there are so few personal rewards in this kind of work, since many women have poured a great deal of their creative energy into it. But it has served to balance for many of them the feelings of frustration which grow from the monotony of their work in the home.

It is possible that we are moving toward an era in which women will have better opportunity to express their creative talents and abilities. There seems to be no indication that women will find this path to expression in the economic enterprise. There will always be a place for women to work in American industry and there will

always be women who want this kind of work. Nevertheless, the most fruitful path seems to be responsibility
for the development of our leisure time. Sometimes,
when pressure of job or committee work has pushed us,
we feel that we have no real leisure. Actually we have a
great deal more leisure than our ancestors, but the pace
of our life is so rapid and the demands on our lives are
so great that we feel harried and pressed most of the
time. We have more leisure now and we shall probably
have a good deal more in the next generation. Much of
this leisure is already allotted to very necessary do-it-
yourself work around the home and care for minor re-
pairs. A good deal of it is also taken up with clubs, committees, church, or union meetings. Nevertheless, there
is still an increasing margin of leisure time which could
be used creatively for the growth and development of
the family. Most of this leisure is being wasted on
second-rate TV programs and third-rate magazines.
Women have a real responsibility here. The planning
and development of evening and week-end activities
which could help the family educationally and culturally
must largely fall to the women. In line with all that has
been said in the preceding pages, it is obvious that this
kind of thing should be planned and discussed with the
man of the house; but, if the woman does not do it, it
will not be done. There are many possibilities for common projects in the family, for creative and interesting
trips, for reading aloud from good books which children
seldom hear these days, and for activities which the family can pursue as a real community. Many women would
feel much freer to develop their interests in this direction if they were not so bogged down in the disciplinary
care of their children. It seems perfectly clear that, as
men take real responsibility in the home, women will
feel more inclined to look to the development of the
family's leisure time.

Several national and international committees have been discussing the role of women in modern life. The existence of such committees implies an uncertainty about woman's role. It would be naïve to claim that there is no problem, and yet there is real danger of exaggerating or confusing the issue. We have already suggested that more than half of the problem is created by men. It should also be added that women are doing a far more significant job than they realize. It helps to balance the picture when we reflect on the contribution of women in our society. If women can assess the value of this contribution, they may feel somewhat less pressed to be "significant." We can limit ourselves here to the work of the housewife, although this should in no way depreciate the contribution of women to teaching, nursing, social work, industry, politics, writing, business, and sundry other activities.

We sometimes forget that very few men earn enough to pay for the work that a housewife does. Widowers with several small children are aware of this fact. Unless they lodge their children with relatives, they can barely manage to rear the children. Cleaning, cooking, mending, nose-wiping, and general care of a house and children make a big job. Pay for this work runs from $3,000 to $4,000 a year, if it is done properly. This is close to the median income of the country. It can, of course, be done for less if the man shares the work. A man puts in a good week's work to earn this much. When suggestions are made about further outlets for female energy, they are not made with a view to creating significance for women. Most housewives match their husbands in productive work essential to daily existence and human life. Many women do find this type of work unfulfilling. Perhaps they forget that their husbands may also be working in jobs which are tedious and personally unrewarding. Women certainly have no reason to feel that their work is productively less significant than their husbands' occupations.

Women also create the fabric of communication and relationship in the community. Their informal relationships are the network of neighborhood community. This is almost too obvious to mention, but it is a crucial role in urban life. Many of our urban areas have very little neighborhood community. This creates innumerable problems for children and parents. In fact, it may turn out that gang problems and racial conflict will not be solved until neighborhood communities can be created. This seems to be the drift of present thinking on these matters. If the adult community does not create an atmosphere of common life in urban areas, the young people roam as anonymous groups in a no-man's land. Men can make a contribution to neighborhood community through P.-T.A., block groups, and informal week-end "palaver." However, the real burden falls to the housewife. One is repeatedly struck with this role of women in the few urban blocks that are acknowledged to have a neighborhood atmosphere. Men enjoy this atmosphere. They use it and benefit from it. They rarely create it. One discovers in these particular blocks a network of female communication which has created a special climate. This is the climate of neighborliness— of knowing one another and being known.

Housewives are significant producers in our society, and they are potentially the living network of such community as we have. Perhaps housewives should consider more carefully their contributions to informal fellowship in neighborhoods. When we take up the development of youth, we shall have occasion to return to this problem. In the context of woman's role, we need think of no other work than neighborliness to see the crucial significance of what women are already doing.

We have been speaking, thus far, about the organization of the family; its system of discipline, division of authority, democratic leadership, and need for outlets. This is really the superstructure of the ship. We look at an aircraft carrier and see its control tower, signal lights, and deck crew. This is merely the superstructure. The superstructure can function successfully as long as the engines are running, crews are at work below decks, and the seams are watertight. This is also true of the organization of a family. We can make minor shifts in the exercise of discipline, who doles out money, who guides the planning of trips, etc. These are all important, because they direct the common life of the family. The real point about a family, however, is what is happening between the people. To use the analogy of the carrier, the problem is what is going on below decks. Husband and wife married because they loved one another. Do they still love one another after these years of marriage? How is their relationship affecting the atmosphere in which the children are growing? Is it a cold and angry climate? Is it honest and loving or are they merely putting up with each other?

The family is above all a personal community. Whatever it may have been in the good old days, it is now *the* personal group in which one can be himself. One can be himself only in a community of mutual trust and love. This is the heart of family living. We cannot create such a community through better organization. In fact, organization is quite beside the point if nothing is done about the personal life of the family group. We consider next this personal aspect of our life together in the modern family.

NOTE ON HUSBAND AND WIFE IN THE BIBLE (see page 53)
In the Bible, authority derives from God. In God, word and deed are one. God spoke and it was so. This is absolute authority. This authority is manifest in the life of the Son, who again points to its

source in the Father. Jesus said to Pilate, "You would have no power over me unless it had been given you from above" (John 19:11). St. Paul says in Romans 13:1, "There is no authority except from God." The authorities of this life, even the rebellious powers of which St. Paul speaks in Romans 8:38, derive their authority and continuation from God. Our Lord defines His mission, and the commission of His disciples in terms of His authority (Matthew 28:18), "And Jesus came and said to them, 'All authority in heaven and on earth has been given to me.'"

The authority in work, government, family, and church is a relative authority, derived from God and held in answerability to God.

The Bible speaks, moreover, of authority *in* community. God is concerned with community—with the togetherness of His people in the power of the Spirit. This togetherness implies a mutual giving which pertains to all the orders of life and in a paramount sense to the family and the Church. This focus on community does not mean that all hierarchy of power, all order of authority and subordination, is done away. Christ exercises His authority through love, but He remains Lord. The apostolic fellowship retains community in Christ and hierarchy of authority under Christ. The tension between these two elements is a commonplace of all life. The tension is never overcome but only deepened in the dissolution of one element or the other. In family life, love and discipline seem to be alternating attitudes of parents to children, whereas the two are really inseparable. Undisciplined love spoils and unloving discipline hardens. Were we not so afraid of authority, we could exercise it more often in love as an expression of love. In Christ we see perfect authority and perfect love united. But now let us consider the biblical ordering of authority in the family.

The father in the Israelite family of the Old Testament held a dominating position and was actually viewed as a source of strength for the whole family and all the blood children. He was, in a sense, possessor not only of his domestic animals and property but also of his wife. The authority and significance of the male in the Old Testament family is generally known and recognized. Even though women had protection of their status and rights, particularly in the earlier period of Israelite history, the figure of the male had predominance with both a social and a religious sanction. Although the New Testament introduces a new element into this picture, there is a real continuity in the New Testament with this view of the role of the father.

The new element introduced into the marriage relationship in the New Testament is the restoration of the dignity and status of woman as a child of God. This is expressed by St. Paul in his letter to the Galatians 3:27–28: "For as many of you as were baptized into Christ have put on Christ. There is neither Jew nor Greek, there is neither slave nor free, there is neither male nor female; for you are all one in Christ Jesus." The New Testament views marriage in terms of a mutuality of love in Christ in which the man and the woman stand together. This is expressed for husbands and wives in Ephesians 5:21: "Be subject to one another out of reverence for Christ." There is, in other words, a recognition that the man *and* woman stand answerable to the Lord for the life in love to which they have been called. The link between husband and wife is Christ, and the form of this link is the relationship of mutual love.

The apostolic church, even as it recognizes this new status of woman, firmly upholds the principle of authority in community and quite clearly in the life of the family. Authority is essential in the structure of community and is given by God. But authority is transformed, even as it is upheld. Many people have felt that St. Paul resented women and was trying to put them in their place. A reading of his letters and of the Book of Acts shows that St. Paul had great appreciation for women's gifts and constantly entrusted them with responsibility. He upholds the authority of the father in the family, but as authority transformed by Christ into a sacrificial care. The domination and arbitrary action of husbands have been done away by Christ. They are to act toward their families as Christ acts for the Church.

Ephesians 5:21–33 is the most developed New Testament passage on marriage and seems consistent with other New Testament teaching. The ordering of authority between husband and wife is stated in verses 22–23: "Wives, be subject to your husbands, as to the Lord. For the husband is the head of the wife as Christ is the head of the church, his body, and is himself its Savior." This implies that the authority given to the husband is to serve as an analogy on earth to Christ's Lordship over the Church. This authority is held, moreover, in answerability to God. The wife is commanded to be subject to the husband, "as to the Lord," which implies that her obedience to the Lord will find expression in her relationship to her husband and that this obedience to the husband should not lead her in any way to transgress her obedience to the Lord. Furthermore, the authority of the husband over the wife and in the family derives from his role as protector and sacrificer for the life of the family. Christ gave Himself for the Church, and so the life of the husband in the family is to be a reflection in its limited way of this pattern of Christ in the Church. By analogy, the wife's role will follow the pattern of the Church in its love and faithfulness to Christ. With all the difficulties of this analogy in Ephesians, the intention of the passage seems clear. Human fatherhood finds its pattern in conformity to Christ's authority and self-giving.

In summary, the pattern of male authority set forth in Ephesians, and we have taken this passage to be at least in line with the development of the Old and New Testaments, is not simply patriarchal nor is it an arbitrarily authoritarian pattern. The Ephesians passage and the Christian view of male authority involve a real ordering of power with a real authority for the husband and father, but it is authority set in a context of mutual love. It is, moreover, a pattern which gives dignity to the woman's role.

The Bible speaks of the authority of the husband over the wife in the marriage relationship, but it treats husband and wife as a unity when it speaks of their authority over the children. This is important in a total Christian view of the family, for husband and wife are "one flesh"—indissolubly united. According to one biblical account, man and woman are created in the image of God in their unity—their relationship (Genesis 1:27). Children are commanded to honor their parents (Exodus 20:12); and in this respect, the parents share the domination (Genesis 1:28). St. Paul similarly assumes the unity of the parents in their exercise of authority over the children (Colossians 3:20).

According to this pattern, the earthly family is an analogy of the relationship of Christ to the Church—an analogous experience in which we can express and experience our life in Christ. Our tendency today is to assume that we can eliminate the authority of husband over wife and yet retain the authority of husband-wife over the children. The Bible is more realistic about marriage than modern man, for the truth is that in dissolving the one hierarchy we destroy the other.

Marriage and the family take on a new and very significant meaning in the life of the community through this analogy to Christ and the Church: all those who live in the family experience the mystery of Christ's love for the Church and for the world; the love of the father for the family cannot be separated from his authority over the family, any more than the love of Christ for the Church can be separated from His Lordship over the Church. The name and pattern of human fatherhood is discerned certainly from the Fatherhood of God, even as the authority of human fatherhood derives from God. But Christ is the revelation of the Father to us and, in Christ's relationship to the Church, we discern the pattern of our human fatherhood. This pattern, moreover, is not a blueprint or a set of formulae. The pattern is actually the expression of the person of Christ which will find its realization in the concrete fatherhood of our own families. We see from Ephesians that this concrete expression will include both hierarchical authority and mutuality of love. Thus, the natural subordination (not inferiority) of wife to husband is transformed *and* fulfilled in Christ. The husband continues as answerable to God for the order and welfare of his family, but the family is no longer his possession to use and enjoy. The family is the place where his ministry of love is to be expressed.

CHAPTER FOUR

THE COVENANT OF INTIMACY

The flowers appear on the earth, the time of singing has come, and the voice of the turtledove is heard in our land.

SONG OF SOLOMON 2:12

It is generally agreed that companionship has become the predominant focus of modern marriage. The family is still the agency that produces children, trains them for life, and shelters them until they are ready to go their own way. Nevertheless, men and women are primarily seeking an intimate relationship in marriage. This has probably always been true but never to the degree that we now experience it. Intimacy is the crucial need in marriage today. It is, consequently, the focus of marital difficulty.

The modern home certainly provides many opportunities for intimacy. The home today usually includes only the husband and wife with their dependent children. It is usually rather limited in space. One architect pointed out recently that we are building smaller and smaller homes while Americans are growing bigger in height and weight. We are certainly thrust together in this modern home. We also have more opportunities for intimacy by virtue of the fact that our work allows more leisure time. This varies with occupations, of course, but the free week-end is not uncommon today. Moreover, there are indications that the working week may soon become even shorter.

The size of the modern family intensifies the inti-

macy of the relationship. A family of five (two parents
and three children) has the possibility of only ten relationships within the family. By contrast, a family of ten,
two parents, six children, and two relatives, has the possibility of forty-five relationships. The smaller family intensifies intimacy by channeling it into fewer relationships. It is like a magnifying glass which focuses the
sun's rays into burning heat. This intensifies intimacy
and limits privacy. *If we mean by intimacy the relationship in which people know one another, support one another, share their lives and identify their interests with
one another, then the modern family can be an extremely intimate group.*

The loneliness of our mechanized way of life creates
intense needs for intimacy. This intimate home is precisely what we want. We have very few personal relationships in work and community, so we put all our eggs
in this one basket. This is *the* intimate group in which
we hope to find personal relationship. Our lodges,
clubs, and associations provide some friendships, but
the coffee house, pub, and cracker barrel are pretty well
gone. This is particularly true for men. Women still
seem to manage some informal gatherings in tot yards,
laundromats, supermarkets, and in "koffee-klatsches,"
but even these groups are transitory. If we can assume
that modern man needs intimacy, we can safely say that
most of us have a big stake in the family.

The restriction of intimacy to the family creates serious problems in marriage. Such a concentration of relationships in narrow confines is always difficult. This was
well portrayed in the *Diary of Anne Frank.* Anne was
confined with her family and a few relatives in a concealed loft. This was their only hope of avoiding arrest
by the Gestapo. In the long months before their discovery, this little group rubbed against one another. Each
petty weakness or eccentricity irritated the others. Ev-

ery fear was accentuated. Every irritation became an occasion for conflict. This book deserves careful reading by the modern family. Apart from its peculiar depth and pathos, it reveals the pressures of excessive intimacy. It reveals the desperate human need for privacy and the inevitable clashes between those who are thrust into overly intimate situations. To be sure, Anne's family was under particular strain, but the situation was in some ways similar to the modern home.

Marriage is intended to be an intimate relationship. This is the one opportunity for sharing one's whole life with another person. To this extent, modern marriage can be a profoundly joyous experience of life together. We should keep this before us as we consider some of the dilemmas created by our overly intimate homes. We may be seeking more from the family than it can provide. We may also be settling for less than the family is intended to be. In this chapter we shall be primarily concerned with problems. In the next chapter we shall consider some solutions.

We shall concentrate in this chapter on the conflict between our need for intimacy and our inability to be intimate. This dilemma of modern man shapes the crises of marriage in our day.

Shrinking Man

Modern life has intensified our need for intimate relationships. It has also weakened our capacity to sustain an intimate relationship. This is one of the fundamental conflicts in modern man. The conflict is created by our way of life, but its greatest impact is felt in the family.

From earliest childhood we are exposed to demands to live up to high expectations. It is not enough for Johnny to be a member of his family. He cannot be just another boy who belongs in the family group. His mother is worried as to whether he is walking sooner or later than Georgie who lives down the street. Is he bigger for his age? Can he read sooner and faster than the other boys? The teacher is always putting up the best papers—Johnny's papers were on the board two weeks in a row. And his father is always asking how he did in sports. Did he sink more baskets than the others? Did he strike out, or was the umpire wrong? How about the scholarship? Did he make it? Certainly, he belongs in this family. Yes, his parents love him. But they love him more when he does well.

The same environment surrounds him as he takes up work. He enters a good plant. He has a *future*. But who is he? He is one more guy who can *do* things—better than some, not as good as others. He is "in" just so long as he can do a little better. He will move up if he follows the leads, keeps in touch with the right people, drops the wrong people, and comes through on that next assignment.

We Americans are doers. We learn from childhood that we can expect love and interest if we can do things. Parents realize that success depends on doing.

This "yardstick rearing"—always putting the measure to children and comparing them with others—does peculiar things to the insides of a person. A child comes to see himself only as a doer—a performer. He is not really a person who wants such-and-such—a person who believes in this or that. He is a bundle of performances which can be called forth by the right signals. He is like a trained dog who gets the signal and jumps through the hoop. A person's insides shrivel in this atmosphere. He becomes more and more anxious about his adequacy. He becomes increasingly worried about failure. A failure is no longer a matter of making a mistake which can be rectified in some way or other. Every failure is a tragedy, because one belongs only if he succeeds.

One must not fail. One has to succeed, because this is who we are—those who succeed.

Successful jobs have always depended upon effective work. This is nothing new. What is *new* in our way of life is the feeling that we only belong as long as we succeed. What is *new* is the sense that we have to be better or get out. Our inner selves become burdened with another self which grows with each new expectation and each new threat to our adequacy. The real self —John, Judy, or Joe—shrinks to insignificance. John struggles to be the person that others expect him to be. His convictions and aspirations are swamped by these outside demands. He changes like a chameleon, adjusting his attitudes and hopes to fit each new group with which he deals. Every personal desire and interest shrink in order to meet the expectations of others. One must be liked. One must be popular. One must fit in. One must get along.

A recent movie was entitled *The Incredible Shrinking Man*. It is the story of a man who shrinks so much that he finally has to fight a spider with a pin. This is a parable of modern man. Man's real self—his personhood as John or Joe—is gradually shrinking. He is shrinking man. Over him towers a self created out of the demands of family, school, friends, and job. He would not shrink if these demands did not threaten the core of his being. His very right to exist as a person is now wrapped up in every new expectation. One really belongs nowhere and to no one. Shrinking man is the prey of anxiety, the victim of loneliness. He feels isolated, because he *is* isolated. He worries about being accepted because he does not feel acceptable. He has to measure up and fit in. If he does not, he will not belong. He no longer knows who he is, since he is only a bundle of responses to the next group he meets. He is only what others expect him to be.

There is a harsh reality to modern industrial life which increases the anxieties of shrinking man. Every step up the ladder of success is marked by increasing pressure to perform adequately. Every step is marked by increasing pressure to fit into the group—to be a member of the team. Attempts have been made to relieve this pressure by seniority in the wage ranks and pensions at higher levels. But there are innumerable ways in which the pressure is sustained. It is harder to fire men in the wage ranks now, but they can be put on undesirable shifts or given isolated jobs. At the higher levels, men can be either by-passed or retired early in order to get them out of the way and make room for more efficient personnel. The fear about adequacy is not imaginary. Procedures are constantly changing. New jobs develop within the organization. Overnight a man is in a new job for which he is not prepared, and he is expected to make the right decisions, move the job ahead and avoid serious mistakes. In most cases it is succeed or be by-passed.

Shrinking man's fears are fulfilled when he is retired early to make room for others. He may retire on a big pension. Presumably life could go on as usual, except that the job is over. But shrinking man has been trained all through life just to work. He belongs to the community so long as he works. This is who he is—So-and-So from Such-and-Such a Company. At retirement he feels that his life is over. This carries over into his personal and social life. His pension is usually too small to carry his family at the level required by his former job. He has to sell and move. Even if he could afford to stay, he is no longer invited to gatherings. He is no longer a useful person to know. He is not even a safe person to know. He does not belong. He is out. Shrinking man can well afford to be anxious. He may fail tomorrow. One can never be this adequate. It is only a matter of time before he makes the mistake of leap-frogging the wrong person or making a really bad decision.

This picture applies somewhat less to women, but it has also had its impact on the inner self of the female in our day. She too has had this pressure to succeed from her earliest days. She too is a shrinking self. She seldom has a real outlet for her performances except in putting pressure on her own children to measure up and succeed. She would probably put somewhat less pressure on her children if she had a real outlet. Since she has no suitable situation in which to be a doer, she may become a perfectionist in her house or reject the home completely. In either case she is shrinking enough to be gloomy and depressed about her situation, seeking some kind of escape and pressing her children to succeed.

Marriage is a haven for shrinking man. It is the one relationship in which one hopes to be loved for oneself. It is the only relationship in which doing can be minimized and being oneself can be maximized. In our day marriage is *the* relationship in which the shriveled self can come to life and grow. It is almost the only relationship in which a person can be loved for himself. It is not easy for shrinking man to accept this kind of love. It is very difficult for him to give this kind of love. And it is no easier for shrinking woman to open her heart with affection and care without regard to her husband's success. Nevertheless, men and women today seek support in the intimacy of marriage as a haven in a very uncertain world. They pour this desperate hope for personal reassurance into the little family group.

The Two Become One

Our way of life not only presses us to seek refuge in the family. It also thrusts upon us the full responsibility for marital choice. Parents, friends, relations, and common background play a very indirect role in marital choice today. The young couple must depend upon their mutual affections and sexual interests to guide them into a wise choice for a lifetime of intense intimacy. As we look at the process of choosing a mate, we see how the excessive need for intimacy is given free play in modern marriage.

Most young people "fall in love" several times before they finally settle on one person for marriage. Parents with teen-age children survive these ups and downs, but it is a harrowing experience. Each month some new "boy friend" is draped on the living-room couch. Each "steady boy friend" brings new interests into the house. It may be "rock 'n' roll" one month and baseball the next. Many a parent today searches his heart in deciding how much the youngster can be influenced in picking and choosing these friends. The girl's parents get the full brunt in the living room. The boy's parents have the anxiety of never really knowing how serious the new date is and not seeing much of her. In either case the parents feel that they have little to say in the choice. An occasional remark may penetrate to the young, but real pressure from the parents seems to have little effect. The basic philosophy, if there is one, seems to be "let them get it out of their systems, so that they can make an intelligent choice for marriage." Roughly speaking, this is the system in the United States.

Obviously this rather haphazard dating process puts a premium on feelings. As young people get beyond high school, they do become somewhat more sophisticated in their choices. Nevertheless, there is quite a bit of pressure on girls to keep up their popularity by going out even when they are not "in love." Every new date holds the possibility of meeting someone else who will be just right. When a relationship becomes really serious, the other dating usually stops. For better or worse, the parents have a new son-in-law or daughter-in-law on their hands. If the choice suits them, they are fortunate. If it does not, they generally try to make the best of it.

It goes without saying that affection and sexual interest are the big factors in this kind of marriage. We have only to think of the Japanese bride of a few years back, whose parents arranged a carefully planned match, in order to realize that our system throws heavy burdens on the capacity of young people to make a good decision. Still more important, our system puts a lot of weight on how the young people feel. Since feelings come and go, many brides and grooms are stricken with doubts just before their weddings. How can you be sure? Is this really the one you love? Young couples have probably always had weak moments just before their marriage, but our system increases the pressure and the uncertainty. The success or failure of the marriage is entirely *their* success or failure. They feel intimate. They love one another. They want to marry and be together without parents trooping through the living room or calling downstairs that it is getting late. But they are doing this on their own responsibility, and it just has to succeed. This just has to work.

Many "viewers with alarm" claim that young people are too casual about marriage. They feel that this generation is headed for marital trouble, because the young people are not "serious" enough. Obviously couples vary in their seriousness about marriage. Nevertheless, most young people seem almost too anxious about the success of their marriages. Some of this anxiety is created by an overdose of adult head-wagging, but most of it seems to come from carrying the full responsibility for the decision.

The anxiety for success in marriage is coupled today with a compulsion to marry as soon as possible. Uneasiness about premarital sexual intercourse may be one

factor in this urge to marry before schooling is over, but
it is probably also stimulated by the excessive loneliness
of people today. Young people are lonely enough already without looking forward to a life alone. Since
World War II the graduate schools of the universities
have been faced with the problem of housing an increasing number of married students. This is not a surprising
trend, but it indicates a deep need to achieve the intimacy of marriage.

This is a tricky combination of forces in a marriage. A
young man feels an irresistible urge to marry. It will be a
long time before schooling is complete or the job is established so that the marriage can be financed. The parents are uneasy about this seemingly premature marriage. The young people have to make the choice on
their own, since that is the way things "should be."
They have read about marital problems. Their marriage
is not going to be like those other marriages. They are
going to be happy. Their marriage *will* be a success.
They hurl themselves into the marriage with a desperate
resolve to be the "happily married couple." They look
forward to inescapable intimacy. They feel "at one" with
each other and they want to strengthen this oneness.

The compound of love and desire with the need for
intimacy forms the base for modern marriage. Newly-
weds enjoy this sharing so much that neither one gets
much privacy for quite a while. If they do not share the
same toothbrush, it is only because the toothbrush is the
last outpost of privacy. The degree of sharing varies with
different people, but intimacy is the dominant note.
This is inevitable when marriage is compounded of the
mixture of love and sexual desire. This combination produces a preoccupation with intimacy—with being at one
in every aspect of life.

Few other societies have rested marriage and family
life on the free choice of young people. The consuming

passion of love, however, is not foreign to other societies and is recognized in the Bible. The Song of Solomon in the Old Testament speaks of it in glowing terms.

> Set me as a seal upon your heart,
>   as a seal upon your arm;
> For love is strong as death,
>   jealousy is cruel as the grave.
> Its flashes are flashes of fire,
>   a most vehement flame.
> Many waters cannot quench love,
>   neither can floods drown it.
> If a man offered for love
>   all the wealth of his house,
>   it would be utterly scorned.
>
> 8:6 f

The Bible also acknowledges the creation of companionship to meet human loneliness—particularly the companionship of marriage. "Then the Lord God said, 'It is not good that the man should be alone; I will make him a helper fit for him'" (Genesis 2:18). The essential place of love and companionship is not alien to biblical thought. In fact, the intimacy of body and mind which means so much in modern marriage is affirmed by the Bible. "Therefore a man leaves his father and his mother and cleaves to his wife, and they become one flesh" (Genesis 2:24). This is the foundation of marriage. Love and sexual desire find their fruition in the intimacy of marriage. The two become one flesh. This is not the whole story of marriage, but it is the first and most important reality about the relation between husband and wife. The time of singing, the romantic passion, is not to be rejected as a passing phase of adolescence. It points to the fundamental reality of marriage— "the two become one flesh." From this day, their lives are committed to one another in the union of one flesh.

They have committed themselves to the intimacy of life together.

In biblical language, marriage is a covenant between a man and a woman. We seldom speak of covenants these days, but this term expresses a unique relationship. We can understand the term most clearly in the light of God's covenant with His people. The Old Covenant is the alliance initiated by God with the Israelite people. The act of God in delivering the people forms the basis of the Covenant. However, the Covenant is sealed by the Commandments and the pledge of fidelity in terms of them from both sides. God promises to be with His people, to empower their obedience to His laws and to protect them. Israel pledges itself to faithfulness to God. Israel will serve no other gods. The history of Israel is the record of God's faithfulness to the Covenant and Israel's struggle with its own mistrust. We need not pursue this further, since we are primarily concerned with the nature of a covenant relationship. Faithfulness, trust, and support are the fabric of a covenant.

The covenant of marriage is only a human analogy to the real Covenant of God. The distinction is important, since God initiates the Covenant with His people whereas man and woman jointly initiate the covenant of marriage. The fabric of the relationship is similar, nevertheless, since husband and wife join in a covenant which excludes other relationships of such intimacy. They pledge faithfulness and mutual trust. They pledge mutual support. They enter into an intimate relationship in which they share their personal and physical lives. They become one flesh.

The marital covenant of biblical times joined many family ties. Political, economic, and religious bonds were cemented through marriage. Families became linked in a complicated network. Family names were continued through significant lines of descent. The marital covenant was a crucial bond in the society. This is rarely true in our day. The marital covenant is now a bond between a man and woman through which a single, intimate family group is founded. The covenant of one flesh is a covenant of intimacy for the husband, wife, and children. They may continue their relationships with parents and relatives, but the pledge of faithfulness and mutual support is limited to the intimate group. This is a covenant of intimacy.

There is a twofold link between God's Covenant with His people and the covenant of marriage. First, God has created marriage for man and bestows His blessing upon it. This means that God promises to support and empower the covenant between husband and wife. He has made them to be one flesh and does not merely leave them to their own resources in the fulfillment of their covenant. Husband and wife continue in the covenant of intimacy with the assurance of God's empowering love. Second, the covenant of marriage is included in the broader Covenant of God with His people. Marriage is not to be a substitute for faithfulness to God and membership in His people. Marriage is not to be man's Church or his salvation. It is not to become an idol. The covenant of intimacy is fulfilled in obedience to God and leads men more deeply into trust in God. If marriage becomes divorced from this broader Covenant, it ceases to be a covenant relationship in the full meaning of the term. There can be contracts between men and women which they make and unmake. A covenant, however, is a unique relationship made before God and empowered by God.

It is difficult to estimate how important intimacy may have been in the marriage of the biblical period. It was clearly a desirable aspect of marriage. There were, however, many other important aspects to marriage in biblical times, and these doubtless took precedence over intimacy. For example, the obligation to perpetuate the family name took precedence over the marital covenant. In our time, the intimacy of personal relationship, mutual sharing and life together, is the real core of marriage. Mutual affection and love are no longer desirable additions to the marital covenant. They are essential functions of marriage. For this reason, we have translated the covenant of one flesh as the covenant of intimacy. Men and women cannot treat the intimacy of marriage as an option in our day. Compatibility, mutual affection, personal responsiveness, and mutual trust are now the essence of marriage. Many other responsibilities accrue to the marital covenant. For example, marriages still bring forth children to whom the covenant of intimacy is extended. But the essence and content of the marital covenant today is intimate relationship. Hence, we shall treat the struggles with marriage in our day in the light of this covenant of intimacy. Success and failure in marriage will be considered in terms of intimacy. The problem of marriage is faithfulness or unfaithfulness to the covenant of intimacy. Since marriage is a covenant and not merely a contract, the problem is also how this faithfulness fits into the broader Covenant of God—how this marriage manifests trust in the promises of God.

Separation or Coexistence

John has been married two years. He likes to read and listen to music. He has been to parties for the last three week-ends and now he faces another round. We see him musing to himself in the living room. . . . "What does Jane think we are, anyway? That whole crowd will be drunk again tonight. Bill thinks he's such a riot after a couple of drinks, so everyone has to hear those stupid remarks. Why should all those guys be hanging around Jane? You'd think she'd have more sense than to encourage that kind of stuff. The rest of that bunch think there's something wrong because I want her to act like my wife. Maybe Bill is right and I'm an old-fashioned so-and-so. Well, I'm fed up. It's about time Jane and I had this out. We're always leaving the baby with some high-school kid. God only knows who that kid has in here while we're out. She gobbles up all the food and drinks all the Cokes. Then she gets all our extra dough for doing nothing. Jane used to be satisfied being with me. Why, at that last party I didn't get a chance to talk to her until we were going home, and then she fell asleep in the car. We saw more of each other before we married. All she thinks about is parties, drinks, and that bunch of heels who think they're such hot stuff. For my money they're just schlemiels. I wonder how Jane would feel if I began paying attention to those gals . . . but who wants to mess around with them? I'm going to put my foot down. After this we stay home and have our week-ends to ourselves. We can take some rides—take the baby along and have some fun together. If Jane doesn't like it, she can lump it. . . . 'What? Yes, I'll be ready in time. No! We won't be late. Yes, I'll get the sitter. Who? Oh, that Seekins girl again—all right. Yes, I know she's dumb, but I'll explain about locking the door and calling us if anything goes wrong. Sure, I'm coming.'"

Is Jane really having such a wonderful time? Not really! She has some thoughts too. . . . "Well, at least we'll be getting out for the evening. If John's doing so well at the plant, why can't we move into a decent neighborhood and get a house I can clean? All he talks about is work, work, work. You'd think he didn't care whether I was here or not. I'm just his maid. Cook, clean up, wash the diapers, cook again. What kind of a mess is this? We used to have fun together. Now, we plan a drive in the car. We're all set to have some fun . . . the baby starts to cry, John gets mad and says it's because we stayed out so late and put her off her schedule. I know we stayed out too late, but at least people were laughing and having fun, instead of talking about work and grouching about the mess in the kitchen. It's easy enough for John to say he wants to stay home. He's gone all day. He never notices me when he gets home. He could just sit in that chair and read all night, but I've got to be up early with the baby. He doesn't know what it is to be inside all day with no company but a baby who can't talk. Sure I like to get out . . . oh, I don't like that crowd any more than he does. . . . So, Bill is kind of a fat slob, but at least he makes people laugh; he enjoys life . . . John has to be so serious, no wonder the crowd thinks he's stuffy. He isn't really, of course, but he always wants to talk about mortgages and cars and stuff, when everyone is set to have a good time. Well, things will be all right when we can move . . . I wonder when John'll get that raise . . . it's been put off twice, but it can't be long now. . . ."

No one is typical. Everyone is a special person with distinctive interests and hopes. Yet John and Jane *are* typical in a way. They have been living on romantic affections built up during their courtship and the first year or so of marriage. The feeling of oneness is rapidly dissolving. Their distinctive interests are surfacing, but they hesitate to face the differences. Why is it that they do not discuss these conflicts? Why is it so hard to face them together? The old glow is off the marriage. The attempts to recapture it by drinking and playing at sex with the gang are not helping. Why are they unable to deal openly with these feelings?

It is difficult to acknowledge conflicting interests when we desperately need the intimacy of a relationship.

If John and Jane have moved around in these first years of marriage, they have few close friends with whom to discuss this growing conflict. They are very much on their own. They are probably clinging closely together in these first years of adjustment. They are trying too hard to keep harmony and adjust to one another's interests. They are looking for more unanimity than is possible for two different people. Each is feeling the need to assert his own interests, and yet each is appeasing the other. This is not what they bargained for.

We shall look at some realistic approaches to this crisis of intimacy in the next chapter, but here we shall consider the escape from crisis. Shrinking man needs an intimate relationship, but he also lacks the personal capacity to share his life with another person. This split in modern man may be overcome, if the need for intimacy keeps him at work on the relationship. For example, John and Jane may begin to air these differences and work through to some reasonable combination of individual life and intimacy. However, they may avoid the crisis completely by ending the marriage. They may also avoid the clash of interests by drifting into separate spheres of life. The reality of a life together can simply go by default. In fact, there is high probability of such an escape from crisis, since modern life will tend to draw them into separate spheres of activity. If the relationships inside the home become fairly tense, it will be natural to drift toward other interests. This is particularly true for men who are interested in their own success.

Some marriages never get off the ground. They end in separation before the couple knows what has happened. This is not a frequent occurrence, but it does happen. The only reason for considering it here is that it sets in relief the precarious nature of modern marriage. Men and women occasionally find themselves married to a person who is quite incapable of maintaining an intimate relationship. Romantic involvements mislead them into expecting a happy marriage with a badly shrunken person. Men and women who are drawn to such people undoubtedly have their own difficulties or they would not get so entangled. However, a young man or woman away at college or working in a strange city may very easily fall prey to such a person.

For example, a young woman married against the advice of her parents. She had fallen in love with a man while they were at college. He was from a different social background, but she loved him and was willing to sacrifice her relationship with her parents in order to marry him. After a long struggle, the parents acquiesced. With this tacit approval, the young woman proceeded with the marriage. It was a simple wedding with few friends. His family lived at such a great distance that they did not come to the wedding. In fact, she never did meet his parents. Her parents were present, but their uneasiness could barely be concealed. In a flurry of rice, the couple went on their honeymoon. After only a few months, they separated. Her husband had offended and degraded her. He had taken to staying out all night without any account of his doings. She needed him deeply, but he was incapable of sustaining a personal relationship. He could accept no real affection. He could give none. Sexual desire had dominated the relationship, and it soon waned.

In this case the woman had never felt any close relationship with her parents. They had been extremely demanding and rarely gave her affection. In their own way they loved her, but in fact they could no more love her than they could love themselves. She felt deeply estranged and alone. She needed the attention this young man had given her. She even needed the careless and dominant way he treated her all through the courtship. She was incapable of a healthy mutuality in the relationship. The hope for oneness was irresistible to her. She sensed that there were many things in the relationship which boded ill for the future, but her needs were too deep to allow such uncomfortable glimpses of reality to enter the picture. She threw herself desperately into this union. She awakened deeply hurt. The marriage had been a nightmare. It was hard to recall why they had married in the first place. Two lonely and shriveled selves had met, united for a moment, and then separated. A desperate need for intimacy is no assurance of a capacity for intimacy. In fact, the more desperate is the need, the less real is the capacity to satisfy it.

In this marriage the shrinking of personhood assumed different forms in the man and the woman. It was this fact which made the marriage a personal disaster. The woman dealt with her isolation by seeking dominating male figures to whom she could submit. This is the loss of selfhood that leads people to submit to mass movements like Nazi racism. In personal relationships it leads to submission to a dominant person. The man, on the other hand, was even more shriveled. He reassured himself about his personhood by dominating submissive women. He was incapable of a personal relationship, so he had to reassure himself through victories in sexual exploit, real and imagined. The need for intimacy haunted every waking moment of their lives. The sense of isolation was handled in different ways by the two personalities, but it poured similar hopes into the relationship. It was no accident that these young people with such different personalities were drawn together. The needs of the one made the other the natural object of desire.

The significance of this tragic marriage is the way in which it reveals the need for intimacy and the incapacity for relationship. Fortunately most people have not been so badly crippled by modern life as this couple. However, we all share partially the inner contradictions within these young people. We also struggle with this desperate loneliness today. We also find the constricting pressures of intimacy a heavy burden. We have been trained for a highly individualized way of life—winning our place through the things that we do. We may be spared the tragic separation of this young couple, and yet we share with them the inner contradiction of modern man. We need intimacy. We are not sure that we can live with it.

Divorce is not the only way in which intimacy is rejected. Many couples simply drift apart. They coexist as long as they can pursue separate lives. Modern life has this effect on marriage. It sets us on different paths. We seldom participate in anything as a family. A man's work places a major part of his life outside the family orbit. Children very soon become absorbed in their school and group activities. Women get caught up in church or community affairs, spending less and less time within the family orbit. We operate as individuals in our society, and we have very few common interests to hold us together. Coexistence is a natural result of our fragmented interests.

If this process of drifting goes very far, families meet only for boring meals or for arguments about money. Such an arrangement may or may not lead to divorce, but it is already a kind of spiritual divorce. It is coexistence, not marriage, and intimacy goes by default. Many couples preserve this coexistence out of habit and for the sake of their children. It is always questionable whether such a barren atmosphere does children more harm than a divorce. At any rate, an illusion of family life is sustained by keeping the members under one roof. The heart has gone out of the marriage, but it may someday revive through a crisis or an awakening.

This design for living is common today. It is amazing

to observe how cleverly coexisting couples keep up appearances. There may be sporadic outbursts of adultery, but these can be hidden with luck. A marriage may seem happy to the outside world. Only a few close friends will be aware of the emptiness in the home. They will see that there is no real love, for there is no relationship.

Coexistence has a real place in marriage, if it is a willingness to let others pursue and develop their own interests. It is when the whole marriage becomes coexistence that it has ceased to be a marriage. The husband and wife pursue their own lives. Each goes his own way. The children find some neutral ground on which to pursue their lives. There is no real hate and no real love. There is little or no feeling of any kind. The house becomes a way station—a place to wait for the car or to pass idle moments. Husband and wife grow apart. They have too little in common to carry on a conversation. They live under the same roof, but they are never really together.

This is the usual way in which intimacy is forsaken in modern marriage. It slips away. At middle life, the husband or wife may awaken to loneliness and pursue another relationship in hope of some satisfaction. Their friends are startled at this "sudden" break in the marriage, because John and Jane seemed so happy. The one who tries to escape this stultifying design for living is treated like a scoundrel, and yet the relationship had ceased to be a marriage years ago. Coexistence had become separate existence.

The Make-Believe Marriage

There is one other escape from the crisis of intimacy which should be mentioned. It is somewhat more subtle than separation or coexistence, but it is a path which modern man is prone to pursue. The escape into a make-

believe marriage and a make-believe family was vividly
dramatized by Arthur Miller in his play *Death of a
Salesman*. This play is a touching portrayal of the way a
man's dream of success can transform family life into
a world of make-believe. Instead of working through the
crisis of intimacy, a man or woman may use his wife
and children to bolster his dream of success. Real relationship and intimacy never exist, but they are imagined
and used as supports for the dream.

The leading figure in this play is Willie Loman. He is
wrapped up in his dream of success. His family does not
fit the dream, so in his imagination he remakes the family. We encounter Willie toward the end of his life. He
is a salesman who has always dreamed of making big
money, but things have closed in on him. It is slowly
dawning on him that his dream will not be realized. He
is no longer selling enough to satisfy his company. He
has even tried suicide on the road several times. However, as his hopes are shattered, he clutches more desperately at the dream.

Willie cannot tolerate anything in his family which
does not fit into the dream. His picture of success includes the happy and successful family. His two sons,
Biff and Happy, are simply average boys. Willie cannot
accept this fact. When Biff has a triumph in football,
Willie has to blow it up to a national success. If the
boys have difficulty in school, Willie has to blame it on
the teacher. Since Willie's dream of success includes the
notion of being popular and well liked, he tends to measure his boys by their popularity. In fact, he has a fantastic picture of their popularity which they can never
contradict. His wife and sons cannot be who they are.
They must fit his dream.

Willie bolstered his dream by an imaginary picture of
his family. He did not see that Happy would never settle
down or do a real job. He could not see that Biff had be-

come a hobo and petty thief. And yet the real tragedy
is that Willie had done a fair job in his work and could
have been a good father. Arthur Miller has undoubtedly
exaggerated Willie's blindness to reality in offering us an
extreme instance for dramatic purposes. Nevertheless,
all of us are blind to circumstances where reality does
not correspond to our consuming passions. We do not
observe the real needs of other persons. We do not accept their limitations. We do not come to grips with
their aspirations. Every person and every reality is somewhat fashioned after our dream. As circumstances contradict the dream, we have no recourse but to move
more desperately into the world of make-believe. As
Willie's family became more and more hopelessly fragmented, he fell entirely under the enchantment of his
illusion about the one happy and successful family.

Even in Willie's case, one discerns possibilities of encounter with reality. Biff was crushed, when he went to
Boston to get help on a school problem and found Willie in a hotel with a woman. Every boy has a somewhat
illusory picture of the superiority of his father, but Biff's
picture had been exaggerated by Willie's fantasies. This
was a catastrophic encounter for Biff. And yet this was
an encounter with reality which was fraught with possibilities. Here, at last, father and son might have faced
facts. This was an occasion for honest confession and
forgiveness. Knowing Willie Loman, we could say that
this was not possible. However, all of us live with dreams
which are shattered on the realities of life. Our failures
and disappointments are often means of looking more
realistically at ourselves and others. Willie could not
face his failure to be faithful to his wife, so he could not
meet Biff in this crisis. He goes his way and the tragedy
unfolds.

Most of us escape the crisis of intimacy by moving
into a less fantastic world of make-believe. We may sim-

ply pursue our own dreams and fail to notice that we are using our families as a support. This is much more common than Willie Loman's world of make-believe. It has, nevertheless, the same effect on the family. No real relationships are possible in such a family, because the family is manipulated and used to bolster success.

Some years ago a woman separated from her husband in rebellion against this kind of manipulation. They had been married for some years. Most of their friends thought they were happily married. He was a man with a promising career. He had benefited from the marriage, because his wife was able to introduce him to important people. She entertained for him. He made a good impression and so they prospered.

It finally dawned on the woman that she was being used. Her husband gave less and less time and affection to her and the children. He worked constantly. Their only friends were business contacts. Their only recreation was on business trips. Her interests were never consulted, her complaints were never heard. Her husband had been affectionate in the first years of marriage, but now he gave her almost no attention.

This couple could have gone separate ways and co-existed. He could have pursued his success, and she could have become absorbed in her children. But even this solution was not a real possibility. Her husband needed her support for his work. He was not content to let her have her own life. He was in the habit of using every friendship for his own purposes. He intended to use his marriage to further his success. His wife, on the other hand, was unwilling to settle for his dream of success. She needed the intimacy of marriage and did not intend to see it evaporate into her husband's work.

In this particular case the couple were reconciled after a few years of separation. Husband and wife were both at fault, and they gradually came to some realization of what they were doing to one another. The complexities of the relationship are not relevant here. This was a typical case of make-believe. No one was more surprised than the husband when his wife left. He could hardly believe it. He had fooled himself right along that they were happily married. He was getting the success that he wanted, and it never occurred to him that there was anything else in life. He had momentarily enjoyed the intimacy of marriage, but it had proved to be an interruption in his path to success.

There are other responsibilities in life besides the intimacy of the marital relationship. Many wives do not realize this. On the other hand, marriage is *the* intimate relationship in modern life, so we have to face the crisis of intimacy or let the marriage go by default. Women are usually more conscious of the importance of intimacy, since they are less likely to be drawn off into work and plans for success. However, a man who does not face this crisis with his wife may never have another opportunity to become a real person.

We have considered some typical flights from intimacy in modern marriage. This makes a rather dismal account, particularly because, at times, everyone flees from intimacy. However, most couples seem to work through the crisis of intimacy. They may escape for a while. They may avoid the clash of interests for a time. They may appease one another or drift apart. Sooner or later, however, the need for a real relationship asserts itself and there is a reckoning. We turn now to that reckoning and some of its possibilities.

CHAPTER FIVE

A TIME TO LOVE

The flight from intimacy is one side of marriage today.
We all flee in different ways from the responsibilities of
an intimate relationship. We want to pursue our own
interests, and these do not always coincide with the interests of others. We want to escape from our responsibilities to husband, wife, or children. Nevertheless, we
need the intimacy of marriage and are usually unwilling to settle for coexistence. We may pursue our own
interests for a time, but sooner or later we come to a
reckoning with intimacy.

This reckoning is the crisis of intimacy. It arises out
of the clash of interests in the marriage. It is the personal
conflict between separate persons who are one. There
are many minor conflicts which do not create a crisis.
They are brushed aside or handled by compromise.
These conflicts do not touch deeply enough to create a
crisis. For example, differences over bedtime, meals, or
expenditures can usually be worked through by compromise. In this way, a crisis is avoided and the marriage goes along peacefully. Some couples undoubtedly
move along in this way to a deep and lasting intimacy
without major conflict. However, the pressures of life
today make it difficult to grow together gradually. We
are more likely to grow apart.

Major crises are common in modern marriage. These
are turning points in the relationship. If the crisis is

successfully resolved, the couple may move toward real intimacy. If the crisis cannot be faced, they may flee from intimacy. This is the real meaning of crisis. It is a dangerous opportunity, when decisions can have fateful consequences.

Conflict over sexual interests is one of the major crises in marriage today. Husbands and wives find this conflict difficult to ignore. Sex seems to be a focus for crisis, because sexual interest is a key factor in romantic marriage. This fact need not imply that sex is the most important aspect of marriage. It is certainly very important, but there are other equally crucial aspects. Furthermore, couples may encounter crises over issues such as authority, the wife's right to work, the husband's preoccupation with his job, or many other aspects of married life. However, these clashes *can* be avoided, so that the intimacy of the marriage never comes into question. The decisive quality of the sexual conflict is that it cannot be avoided and brings intimacy into question.

We must deal with the sexual conflict in general terms, since its particular manifestations vary from marriage to marriage. There is, however, a certain uniformity in the way it arises. Furthermore, we can assume that the resolution of this conflict will not be too different from the resolution of other conflicts. We take the sexual conflict as representative of the many other ways in which the crisis of intimacy arises. The sexual conflict is, after all, usually a symptom rather than a cause of difficulty in the marital relationship. Since the romantic marriage rests on sexual attraction, it is almost inevitable that sexual difficulty will be the symptom of its breakdown. Couples who deal honestly with this conflict have to face the character of their relationship. In this way they come face to face with the meaning of love in marriage.

The Sexual Conflict

The Kinsey studies of sexuality have made it quite apparent that we have several patterns of sexuality in America. The central pattern and the one that is becoming increasingly common results in a specific type of conflict. The male has a strong need for sexual satisfaction. The female may have this need in the first years of marriage, but she soon loses interest. In fact, many women become almost frigid after a few years of marriage. Men, on the other hand, become more compulsive in their need for sexual satisfaction. As the man goes up in his sexual interest, the woman goes down. There are a considerable number of women who never gain sexual satisfaction in marriage, which is a different though related problem. The peculiar fact is that many women who enjoy sexual intercourse in the early years of marriage gradually lose interest.

Many reasons have been advanced for the sexual conflict in marriage. The usual reasoning is that men have more sexual vitality than women. There may be some basis for this, but it could never be proved, since our sexual attitudes are shaped largely by our way of life. How much of this problem centers in physiological vitality and how much is simply the pressure of marriage could never be absolutely determined. Nevertheless, there are two good reasons to believe that difference in sexual vitality is a minor factor. One reason for discounting the physical factor is the fact that many women enjoy sexual relationships in the early years of marriage and yet gradually become unresponsive. Another reason is the fact that many women regain their enjoyment of sexual relationships after they have worked through the personal aspects of the marital relationship.

There is no question that the care of children drains

the emotional responsiveness of women today. We have already considered some of the conflicts in child care, and these undoubtedly have repercussions on sexual activity and interest. Mothers too easily become entangled with children in emotionally exhausting relationships. This is a trademark of the overly intimate home. The husband's sexual demands soon become merely one more demand. Moreover, modern methods of contraception make it difficult for the wife to protect herself from these demands on the ground that she already has too many children. She can only reject the demands on the grounds that she is tired, uninterested, or disturbed about some problem. In any case, her inability to respond calls into question her womanhood. In fact, it calls into question the one feature of her existence which our society covets—her ability to attract and interest the male. Whatever excuses she makes, her inner confidence is shaken by the fact that she feels sexually inadequate.

Women undoubtedly suffer emotional exhaustion from children these days. The cause for this is not necessarily simple. In fact, the wife may be exhausted by her children, because she has substituted them for her husband. The wife may turn more and more attention to her children, as her husband turns his attention away from the marriage. She may seek the intimacy of marriage in her relationship with her children. This in turn puts a heavy burden on the children, since they are not emotionally prepared to meet these demands. In fact, the demands are quite inappropriate, since the children are not married to their mother. This excess of maternal attention makes the children rebellious one moment and angelic the next. They are afraid to escape the mother for fear of losing her affection. At the same time they want nothing more than to hide from her, because she is absorbing their lives. Such a twisted relationship can easily exhaust the woman, so that she cannot respond to her husband. This is only one possible interpretation of the emotional exhaustion of the wife. It does occur, however, and arises with the breakdown of intimacy in the marriage. According to this interpretation, the sexual conflict has its real roots in the breakdown of intimacy in the marriage. The excessive involvement with the children arises from a need for intimacy with the husband. It leads in turn to a lack of emotional energy to respond to the husband.

There is, of course, a natural decline in the romance of marriage with the arrival of children. The romance becomes routine. Husband and wife make a transition from involvement with one another to preoccupation with work, diapers, cleaning a house, and making their way in the world. They find less and less time for one another, as they are increasingly occupied with their children. The wife is confined to the house with two or three children. Opportunities to get out with her husband diminish. Her romantic relationship with her husband has dissolved into the routine of married life. Marital intimacy built on a romantic relationship is bound to be shattered by routine. Marital intimacy has to find a deeper foundation if it is to continue as the heart of the marriage.

This breakdown of romantic intimacy is aggravated today by the kind of male our society produces. Presumably a marriage would move from romantic intimacy to a deeper, personal intimacy in the course of marital life. Unfortunately men today are not prepared for the deeper levels of personal intimacy. This is *the* characteristic of "shrinking man"—he hides his feelings and avoids personal intimacies. The struggle to be adequate forces him to hide his feelings. He cannot show fear or uncertainty. Any lack of confidence is a sign of inadequacy. In hiding some feelings he finds himself hiding all feelings. The more competitive his work becomes, the colder he grows. We hide our feelings in order to appear adequate. We avoid intimacy in our work, because friendships can shackle us as we try to move up the ladder of success. Soon we do not have to hide the feelings, since we no longer feel anything about people or things. We cannot cry and we cannot really laugh. We become coldly efficient.

With the breakdown of romantic intimacy, the wife seeks personal intimacy in mutual concern, affection, and attention. These are precisely the kinds of intimacy for which the male is least fitted. His inability to meet this expectation brings into question his adequacy as a husband. He has been touched at the vital point—his adequacy. He responds by further sexual demands, since he can reassure himself about his masculinity through sexual activity. The wife's womanhood is now in question, since she is seeking a more personal intimacy and cannot feel responsive to these sexual advances. The man's masculinity is in question, since he cannot arouse a sexual response and feels inadequate to personal intimacy. He does not dare let himself feel his joys, angers, fears, and hopes. The real issue is personal intimacy, but the symptom is sexual conflict. Moreover, sexual conflict is *the* symptom of the breakdown of intimacy because of the special character of the sexual act.

Sexual intercourse is not only a physical act. It is not simply a matter of relieving certain physiological tensions. Every human act expresses feelings, attitudes, and concerns. We put an arm around a friend in trouble, or hold a child to comfort him. These physical acts are primarily important because of the concern and feeling which they convey. This is even more true of sexual intercourse. The sexual act conveys solidarity, intimacy, mutual concern, and surrender to one another. It expresses intimacy in the fullest and deepest sense. The breakdown of intimacy in marriage empties the sexual act of its substantial meaning. Sexuality without mutual intimacy is counterfeit. It is like using bad money. When there is no guarantee of validity behind currency, people know they have been cheated by a counterfeiter. This is the character of sexuality without intimacy. It is counterfeit. It pretends to symbolize attitudes which do not exist. Romantic intimacy has dissolved and no deeper level of intimacy has appeared. Counterfeit sexuality becomes more and more distasteful to the wife, since it does not meet her need for personal intimacy. She senses the hollowness of the sexual act. Sexuality becomes a means of reassurance for the man under the threat to his adequacy, but he too senses the counterfeit quality in his sexual interest.

It would seem that sexual activity should be dropped until personal intimacy has been restored, but there is another side to this problem. Human acts convey meanings and attitudes, but they also create attitudes. Every human act has this double character. Putting an arm around a friend in difficulty conveys our concern. It also increases our concern. We create attitudes by what we do. We express attitudes by our acts. Both things are true. Consequently sexual intercourse is not simply an expression of intimacy. It is a means of deepening and strengthening intimacy. A husband kisses his wife to express his closeness to her. He also creates a deeper intimacy with her by kissing her. Therefore, one cannot simply drop expressions of intimacy in hopes that one will some day feel intimate. We are physical creatures who live and grow through the physical things that we do. We cannot maintain friendships without seeing, visiting, and corresponding with our friends. A husband and wife do not become intimate without physical acts of intimacy and mutual concern. In the midst of the sexual conflict, husbands have an obligation to limit

their sexual demands, particularly because they often
make these demands without really feeling a desire for
sexual intimacy. They know the counterfeit character of
much of this sexuality. On the other hand, wives have a
real obligation to make a serious effort at sexual response. Sexuality expresses intimacy. It also creates it.
We discover deeper levels of personal intimacy through
expressions of intimacy, although we are constantly in
danger of using our expressions as counterfeits for the
real article.

Life against One Another

We asked in the last chapter why John and Jane, like so
many other couples, find it difficult to discuss their conflicts today. Why is it so difficult to work out these differences? Why do so many couples consult the divorce
lawyer without ever having talked through their problems? One aspect of this is the fear of conflict. Perhaps
the pressures of modern life have made us feel so hostile
that we are afraid to show any hostility. There is always
the possibility that we shall show too much. This is
connected with the coldness of trying to be adequate.
We hold back feelings until we can express neither joy
nor anger. (We shall not discuss here those families that
are always bickering and fussing and those that are constantly angry about something. Theirs is a very special
problem and they are not really facing differences, or re-
solving anything. The more usual pattern is to hide
hostility until it finally bursts forth and blows the roof
from the house.)

Most families today need more honest conflict and
less suppression of feeling. Families that hide their differences run the risk of conflicts which are too disastrous.
There are obviously proper times and occasions for conflict. No one benefits from the random expression of

hostile feelings. There are, however, occasions when differences need to emerge. Most couples know when, how, and where such things should be faced.

We cannot find personal intimacy without conflict. Intimacy and conflict are inseparable in human life. This is true in the relationship between God and man. It is true in human relationships. God makes demands on us which limit our control over life. We want to say what is good and bad, as it suits our interests, position, and aspiration. God sets limits over our interests. The story of the Rich Young Man in the New Testament reveals this constant conflict between the demands of God and human aspirations. The Rich Young Man lived a moral life, and Jesus "looking upon him loved him . . ." He was a "good" man by human standards. Then Jesus said to him, "You lack one thing; go, sell what you have, and give to the poor, and you will have treasure in heaven; and come, follow me" (Mark 10:21). Every person has invested his security in the possessions, capacities, relationships, or memberships which he has. These differ with people but the fundamental problem is the same. We invest our lives in the things that *we* possess. We cannot enter into the life with God so long as we worship this particular investment. God demands the surrender of this investment, since our relationship to Him cannot be secondary to any human interest or possession—wife, money, position, or ambition. The Rich Young Man's heart sank at the prospect of giving up the prestige, security, and control which his money assured. He went away sorrowful. Jesus said nothing about the goodness or badness of money, position, or ambition. Again and again He confronted people with their worship of things other than God; money here, Temple practices there, legalistic obedience for some, unscrupulous dealing for others, etc. At every point along the way, Jesus engaged men and women, authorities and beggars, in the conflict. Some went away sorrowing. Others plotted and disposed of this troublemaker who brought their idols into question.

We limit one another in a less decisive way than God limits us. Nevertheless, intimacy leads to conflict, because our differing interests clash and limit the selfish pursuit of our own lives. Since we resent the ways in which others limit and circumscribe our lives, the resulting conflicts are often cruel and angry. This is one reason why we fear conflict in marriage. The feelings run too deep. The resentments are too strong. We dare not risk the rift in the marriage that may follow an expression of feelings. Nevertheless, personal interests must be confronted, if personal intimacy is to emerge. Love and conflict are inseparable.

John and Jane are in for some hard days as they face some of their differences. Jane will find it difficult to accept criticism of her flight from housework and her children. John will be shocked at his wife's resentment of his lack of interest and inability to express any real concern for her or the children. Trivial conflicts will develop into intense arguments over a multitude of issues. John has his own life. He must pursue his job. On the other hand, he has bound his life to Jane, and she has legitimate claims on his time, attention, and personal affection. John cannot meet these expectations according to his own whims. He is answerable to another person in the fullest intimacy of life together.

The tragic character of much marital conflict is that it explodes after years of suppression. Some trivial incident triggers off pent-up feelings and all hell breaks loose. The husband may start this over the wife's purchase of a new hat or her decision to go to an organization meeting. The wife may start it over the purchase of a new fishing rod. Suddenly the roof falls and the couple is caught in a series of explosive battles. Recriminations,

bitterness, hatred, and even violence may accompany
this outburst. Feelings of resentment, too long suppressed, suddenly surface and surprise the couple with
their fury. This is the result of years of appeasement.
Neither partner has been willing to express real differences. The pressure cumulates in the boiler. Finally the
valve blows and the house is full of steam.

Conflicts that have been suppressed too long are hard
to resolve. When the feelings come into the open, it is
impossible to distinguish real from imagined hurts.
Neither partner can distinguish his own or the other person's just complaints. The house is so clouded with
steam that husband and wife cannot see the real issues.
In this mixture of real and unreal charges, cruel things
are said which are hard to forget. Steps are taken which
are not easily retracted. Such a struggle can go on for
months like a fire set in a dry heath—smoldering and
then breaking again into flame. Such conflicts end up in
divorce courts more often than not. Too many years of
suppression had blocked the possibility of engaging in
an honest confrontation with differences.

Obviously a third party is essential to reconciliation
in such long-delayed outbursts. Couples too seldom
turn to pastors or family counselors for help when
caught in the web of past hurts. Sometimes a divorce
lawyer proves a last-minute resource by helping a couple
clear the air and face their differences in the last stages
of such a battle. The significant thing about these experiences with third parties is our human need for objectivity in the midst of conflict. We become so deeply
enmeshed in defending ourselves that the other person's
interests are obscured. The third party introduces a note
of objectivity. A husband can make extravagant charges
against his wife to another person without any objective
check. He can even criticize his wife extravagantly to her
face. The situation changes, however, when a neutral

friend or pastor sits by while husband and wife exchange their differences. The third party does not have to interfere. He has only to be there in order to introduce a note of objectivity. Husband and wife will both look to him for justification and approval. If he remains neutral but concerned, they soon begin to look a little more honestly at their charges in order to test their justification.

Marriages seldom mature into life together without the help of a friend, relative, or pastor. We all need friends and groups with whom to share in confidence. Our lack of trusted friends is partly a consequence of our mobile way of life. It is also partly our own fault. Many of us are unwilling to confide our failures to anyone—even a pastor or relative. We feel that we must be adequate to everything, and it is difficult to admit failure even to trusted friends. Suffice it to say that long-delayed conflicts can shatter a marriage unless a third party can be introduced.

If personal interests and differences have to be hidden beyond a certain point, there is no exit from mere coexistence. The web of circumstance will hold us in parallel paths which never intersect. Husband and wife depend on the power of love to carry them through the inescapable conflicts of intimate relationship. They depend also on past experiences of joy and suffering. They have, after all, been through many things together. It has not all been romance. They also depend upon their commitment to one another—their pledge to support one another through the sickness and health of life. However, past experience and commitment quickly fade out of sight in the midst of conflict. The real power to survive conflict is love. Love is the power of life together and the source of life for one another. It is the only solution to the crisis of intimacy. Conflict helps us face the crisis, but only love can carry us through it.

Life for One Another

It has often been noted that six "persons" are involved
in every marital relationship: the husband as a person,
the husband as he imagines himself to be, the husband
as the wife pictures him, the wife as a person, the wife
as she imagines herself to be, and the wife as her husband pictures her. Put in this way, the problem of love
in marriage is to bring the two real persons into a life
together. Since the imaginary persons are created by the
needs of husband and wife, both partners strive constantly to fit the other person into the suitable image.
Since the image seldom fits the other person's character and aspirations, it takes a long time for the true
identities of the partners to emerge. For example, a husband may think of his wife as the placid provider of
food. He needs this picture of a maternal companion to
comfort and reassure him. His wife, in fact, is a flighty,
joyous creature who occasionally prepares a special
meal for fun but is bored to death by cooking. The husband probably enjoys these characteristics in the wives
of his friends. He cannot tolerate them in his wife. The
work of love is to bring the husband into loving encounter with the real person of his wife. This is intimacy.

We do not escape the world of make-believe by accident. There are definite commitments and decisions
in marriage by which we create a situation for love.
These decisions are largely within our power. In the
crisis of intimacy, we face two crucial decisions. The first
is to listen to the other person. The second is to stand
together in the relationship. These are actually repeated
decisions, and they create the situation in which love
can enter a marriage.

The decision to listen to the other person is crucial to

a covenant relationship.* Faithfulness to the covenant involves willingness to listen, to hear, and to heed. This is not easy to do, because we unavoidably encounter the real claims of the other person when we listen. We have to deal with the real person. We can only escape the world of make-believe by listening to the other person. We enter intimacy with a real person when we hear him. We cannot enter personal intimacy without giving attention to the other person.

The decision to listen is, therefore, a willingness to be present. We are physically present in many contacts with people, and yet we are seldom personally present. Physical presence is not necessarily personal presence. If I look at my wife, I can see her. If I speak to her, she may or may not answer. If she asks me a question, I may answer absent-mindedly or attentively. My mind may be wandering over the day's work or to an anticipated game of golf. I am physically present, but I may not be personally present.

We say today that we have "no time"—we are busy. Husbands and wives often complain that they have little time together. The question is, what do they do with the time that they do have? Are they personally present when they are together? Our way of life thrusts our attention on the future—anticipated difficulties, purchases, changes, and fulfillments. This anticipation of the future thrusts us out of the present. We may be physically present, but our minds are turned to the future.

We cannot hear the other person unless we are personally as well as physically present. Many husbands ob-

* This note is sounded again and again in the Bible in the relationship of God's people to their Lord. "Hear, O Israel." They heeded God or they did not heed Him. Jesus is described in the Gospel of St. John as the Word of God. Jesus tells His disciples, "He who hears you hears me . . ." (Luke 10:16).

ject that their wives carry on a running chatter about trivialities, so that they lose their minds if they have to hear it. There is probably some truth in this. We use up another person's attention if we insist on bombarding him with trivialities. But it is not always easy to judge what is trivial. Many husbands get in the habit of ignoring their wives' chatter. However justified this may be on occasion, such chatter often conceals a real attempt to share serious concerns.

Unwillingness to listen is a decision in favor of the imaginary picture of the other person. Unwillingness to listen is a way of avoiding impressions which might shatter that picture. Intimacy requires repeated decisions to listen, to be attentive, and to be personally present.

Prayer is closely related to listening and being present. We often begin to hear others by praying for them. These prayers may be momentary requests for God's help. They may be a part of the regular process of our nightly prayers or Sunday worship. God's answer to our prayers may come in the opening of our ears and eyes. We may see in a moment the way in which we have turned aside from this person. We seem to hear him for the first time. We see her in a new light as someone who has her own life.

We can decide to stand together. This is faithfulness to the covenant of intimacy. Willingness to stand together is a second human contribution to the working of love. It is easy to stand together when things are going well. We are enjoying one another. We like the house and neighborhood. The children are getting along well in school. Life seems perfect. Then, the wife is ill and unable to carry her share of the load. Or worse still, the husband is ill and in a continual grouch over being in bed. Nothing is right. He expects constant nursing in this terrible illness. His wife has a house to clean and children to bathe. She either gives too much attention or not enough. Even these matters are trivial compared to the discovery that we dislike one another as well as love one another. Sulky silences are infuriating. Constant fear of having done the wrong thing seems so stupid. We love one another and yet we dislike so many things about one another. These discoveries are not as difficult as the digs at vulnerable points. Intimacy brings sensitivity to the weak spots in the other person. These vulnerable points are jabbed when feelings are hurt. We have never really been hurt by another person until we have been intimately tied to someone. But even these conflicts of intimacy are not so hard to bear as the boredom of a relationship which has come to mean nothing. It seems foolish to stand together through boredom. Conflict is at least a sign of life. Boredom is a sign of death. Surely this marriage has served its purpose and had better be ended. And finally there are the irreconcilable differences in temperament and interests. Such differences can lead to bitter and continuing conflict. At these points it is extremely difficult to stand together. These are the moments of decision.

We stand together without knowing what good can come from such perseverance. The relationship seems hopelessly inadequate and confused. We are getting so little satisfaction out of it. Every reasonable judgment says to be done with it. We may not wish to separate, but we are impelled to withdraw from the conflict. Each person has his own way of withdrawal. Some sink into silence. Some become violently angry. Others get out of the house and return when quiet is restored. Others seek new relationships to comfort them. If we decide to stand together, we do so without seeing the consequences.

We realize the difficulty of standing together when we see a couple in the face of adultery. The violation of chastity is one problem in adultery. The rejection of the other person is an even more difficult problem. In fact, adultery has this character of "getting even"—of showing up the inadequacy of the other person. If we think in terms of justice, we do not expect a husband to stay with his wife if she has committed adultery. He may feel no willingness to forgive—no capacity to love. He is simply resentful. He does have the power, however, to stand with her in hope that something may come of this relationship. The decision to stand together is made in hope, but it is our decision.

We need not argue whether listening and standing together in a covenant relationship are human or divine decisions. God certainly strengthens and confirms us in these decisions through His Spirit. His reconciling and uniting power pervades all of life and reality. His Spirit holds all life together. Nevertheless, we are free to turn toward the other person or away from him. God confirms man in this freedom, because God takes human decisions seriously. Our decisions have consequences for our marriages. These two decisions are crucial to the covenant of intimacy and we cannot escape responsibility for making them. We can listen and we can stand together. We can make this contribution to love in marriage.

God works through our decisions. He gives love to a marriage. His love fulfills the covenant of intimacy. His love comes as acceptance and forgiveness. God brings *acceptance of the other person* through our listening and standing together. This is one form of love. A husband listens to his wife and gradually discovers that she is a flighty, irresponsible person. He knew this deep in his heart all the time, but he never really admitted it to himself. He simply could not accept this real person whom he had married. In listening to her and standing with her through these flights of irresponsibility, he begins to find a new relationship with her. He begins to acknowledge that this is who she is. She may change and she may not. He is not merely tolerating her. He is loving this person, this wife. He sees here someone whom God loves and cherishes. He now begins to reveal himself to her as *he* really is. Some of the pretense slips away. The relationship takes on some reality. He begins to find a capacity to accept himself through his acceptance of her. He can live with himself without pretending, because he can live with her without making her into someone else.

If we know ourselves at all, we realize that we are neither adequate nor acceptable. We fall short of what we know we could be. We fail in our responsibilities. We do not listen to others. If we do listen, we really do not want to meet their demands for concern. We have too many other things to do. We just wish they would go about their business. To be sure, we respond some of the time. If we look back on those moments, we can be cynical and say that it was because we were in a good mood. The point is that it is hard being what we are. With this self-awareness, it is unbelievable that we should experience acceptance by a person who knows us well. Acceptance in marriage is acceptance by someone who knows us. A wife comes to know her husband pretty well. She sees his failings and his strengths. She could give a fair estimate of his prospects. Acceptance by her can free him from the burden of his inadequacies, because he realizes that he can be loved as he is. He knows what it means to be loved for himself. He begins to understand what it means to love oneself, for he has experienced being loved. He has revealed himself in intimacy to his wife and been received in love when he feared rejection. He can live with himself, because she can live with him. He feels accepted and can begin to accept himself. He can cast away some of the pretense. He can be himself.

We need not defend God by saying that this is a gift of God. Those who find in themselves the power to accept in this way have every right to take the credit. We should remember, however, that acceptance in an unequal relationship—doctor and patient, pastor and parishioner, counselor and counselee, etc.—is different from acceptance in a marriage. The accepting pastor is still the pastor. Husband and wife, on the other hand, are equals. They are peers. Both have a stake in the marriage. Each is hoping for the best partner in marriage that life could have provided, whereas the psychiatrist only has a job so long as his patients have problems. Acceptance in marriage is the power to love someone and receive him in the very moment that we realize how far he falls short of our hopes. Acceptance in marriage is love among equals. It is love between two people who see clearly that they do not measure up to one another's dreams. Acceptance is loving the real person to whom one is married. Acceptance is giving up dreams for reality.

God also brings forgiveness into marriage. We see this most easily in cases of adultery and disloyalty, but it is really the daily bread of married life. Forgiveness is the fabric of all human life together. Most of us can only forgive conditionally in the affairs of life. We can forgive deceit, if there is some assurance that it will not be repeated. We can forgive an outburst of unjustified hostility, if there is some indication that the other person intends to curb his feelings. We are often involved in forgiving *on condition* that the other person sincerely intends to do differently. The more serious the injury, however, the more difficult it becomes to forgive. Then we encounter rejections, deceits, disloyalties, and hostilities which we are incapable of forgiving. At these points we are helpless before our own feelings.

The experience of forgiveness within a relationship transforms these absolute rejections. The adulterous husband may be penitent. If he is, his wife may find it easier to forgive. This, however, is conditional forgiveness. The real rejections come as we justify ourselves for our acts against the other person. Then the wife finds herself helpless to forgive. She has no assurance that things will be different. Her husband may do the same thing tomorrow. On the other hand, he will continue to defend himself unless her forgiveness releases him from the need to vindicate himself.

In the hurts and disloyalties of marriage, we find ourselves unforgiving. We are driven back on elementary faithfulness to the covenant. We can strive to hear the other person. We can attempt to listen and know what is in his heart. We can stand together even though it seems senseless to continue the relationship. We begin to discover the many things for which we must be forgiven daily if we are to have life together. We discover that we are living every moment by the forgiveness of others. We receive a power to forgive hurts without any assurance of amends. A wife begins to realize that it is her own unresponsiveness which contributed to her husband's adultery. She sees her own need for forgiveness as she forgives.

Thus forgiveness is also a relationship between equals. This seems absurd at first glance, since one person has been offended and the other has done the offending. The offending one is the culprit. The offended wife stands above her disloyal husband and forgives with condescension. What relationship could be more unequal than this? Such unequal forgiveness is not, however, the real forgiveness of love. Real forgiveness constitutes the intimacy of equals. We cannot be intimate in unequal relations. One is not intimate with a king. In marriage, each senses his need for forgiveness. Each is grateful for the forgiveness of the other. Since human intimacy assumes equality in the need for forgiveness, no intimacy can come from condescending forgiveness. This accounts for the hopeless way in which most families cope with an alcoholic member. The alcoholic repeatedly throws himself on the mercy of his family. They regretfully forgive his weakness. Until they can enter into his weakness in some appreciation of their own need for forgiveness, the relationship continues in inequality. He is bad. They are good. This is precisely the distortion in the relationship that his weakness seeks to perpetuate. He wants them above him. He can only be saved in discovering that they really see themselves with him. They forgive as a token of the fact that they know how deeply they need forgiveness.

Forgiveness brings equality into the covenant of intimacy. It brings mercy and gratitude. This is the essence of love—the giving of unearned gifts out of gratitude for life together. When husband and wife experience this quality of life together, they have received the gift of love and entered into personal intimacy. Romantic intimacy has dissolved in the routine of life. Childish things have been put away. The real intimacy of acceptance and forgiveness has been received. The covenant of intimacy has become the covenant of thanksgiving. This is God's fulfillment of the human covenant.

Truth can be spoken in love, when husband and wife are bound together in forgiveness. There will still be conflicts, hostilities, loneliness, and disloyalties—real or imagined. The beginning of a new relationship is not an eternal dose of tranquilizers. Much truth will be spoken in heat and rejection. Certain weaknesses will repeatedly confront husband or wife with the problem of acceptance. There is no once for all in human life which moves us to a plane above the struggle of human interests and fears. Forgiveness will continue to be the only possible basis of intimacy. Nevertheless, the reality of this relationship can mature under these conditions. There can be mutual discovery of the real persons.

There can be an honest mixture of coexistence and life together. Another person's right to privacy and personal interests can be respected. A capacity to listen and to be personally present can develop. Depressions and anxieties may not disappear, but they can and do diminish.

The covenant of intimacy is fulfilled through acceptance and forgiveness. Real persons in relationship emerge. Conflicts continue, but they occur in the context of a relationship which can hold them. We are repeatedly thrown back upon elementary faithfulness to the covenant. Persons grow and change. We feel that we have others pigeonholed and suddenly they have grown out of our neat categories. We discover that we must listen to them in order to know who they are and where they are going. We encounter new things in the other person which are unacceptable. Now, however, a level of personal intimacy has been reached on which personal lives can be built. Sexual conflicts may continue, but the tensions in sexual relationship begin to make sense. We become aware of the effort required to maintain an intimate relationship. We begin to see that our own personal lives can only grow as we make these efforts and live with others who accept and forgive us. The crisis of intimacy sometimes looks like the end of the marriage. When we are faithful to the covenant, this crisis becomes the beginning of the marriage.

Personal intimacy is not simply a matter of attitudes. Love appears as acceptance and forgiveness, but it issues in different ways of acting. We do things for one another. New actions issue from God's fulfillment of the covenant of intimacy. Money may be distributed differently. Children may be given more attention in some cases and more privacy and freedom in others. Wives begin to include their husbands in the responsibilities of the family. Husbands gain freedom to accept this responsibility and to receive guidance from their wives in understanding the children. Personal intimacy involves actions as well as feelings. Love leads to imaginative handling of situations, new insights about responsibilities, and new ways of dealing with one another. This almost goes without saying, but we sometimes forget that love is an active power expressing new ways of life together.

The development of democratic leadership in the family is not possible without intimacy. A husband will not even see his failure as a father unless he listens seriously to his wife. A woman cannot support her husband in the assumption of authority unless his acceptance frees her from the need to prove her significance. Democratic leadership and life together can emerge in the modern family, but they cannot emerge separately. They are interwoven strands of the new pattern of family life. If we decide for life together, we shall find ourselves driven to decisions for a creative pattern of responsible leadership. Love brings new life to all aspects of a marriage. Love frees us to be real persons and to live intimately with the other persons to whom we are committed in life together. Love frees us to live *for one another*. The crises of intimacy are a time to love. They are the breaks in flight which bring the covenant into question. They are simultaneously the opening of the relationship for the gifts of love. God acts in our weakness to fulfill the covenant according to His promise.

CHAPTER SIX

YOUTH IN TRANSITION

A few years ago some teen-agers drove hurriedly through the streets of Chicago. They were out to avenge a member of their gang. As they drew alongside a curb where some young men were lounging and chatting, several of the boys jumped from the car to look over the group. One of the gang sat in the car with a rifle pointed through an open window. He fired point-blank at one of the street-corner boys and killed him. The gang escaped but were later apprehended by the police.

The boy who fired the rifle is now in prison and may be there for life. He described the incident as an "unfortunate" accident. It was a case of mistaken identity, completely pointless from the gang's point of view. The young killer still finds it difficult to understand why so much was made of the incident. "It was an unfortunate accident and too much has been made of it."

Such incidents are not confined to Chicago. They are becoming commonplace in every city in our country. The incidents range from petty stealing and vandalism to killing. Violence occurs between gangs. It strikes the bystander, the youngster hurrying to his paper route, the storekeeper, the policeman, and the teacher. Violence is more common in depressed neighborhoods, but it is not confined to the underprivileged groups. The nation has been repeatedly shocked in recent years at the extent of violence among privileged youth. The antisocial behavior of the young ranges through every district and over every class boundary of urban life.

The conflict between youth and the standards of society is most evident on the highways. Drag racing, "peeling," and "chicken" are terms which symbolize reckless adventuring on the highways. Many adults look calmly at these dangerous games and say that they are merely a way of sowing wild oats. This may well be. However, our highways are crowded with pedestrians and powerful automobiles. There is no hiding place. The young brave is no longer showing his valor by stealing a horse from a neighboring tribe. He is not appearing in camp with the scalp of an enemy. He has just sent an old man from the neighborhood to the hospital with a broken back. The young are turning against their own flesh and blood.

The revolt of the young is most evident in the schools. One of Detroit's outstanding teachers regretfully retired from teaching a few years ago. She had found herself more and more occupied with keeping a modicum of discipline in the classroom so that serious teaching was hardly a possibility. If there is a revolt of the young, the classroom is the inevitable point of outbreak. The teacher represents the expectations and standards of the society. Conflict with these expectations is, therefore, bound to be vented on the teacher. It is not surprising that gangs have a high record of violence against teachers and school principals. The teacher is the symbol to youth of what the society demands.

This picture of the revolt of youth should not be exaggerated. The majority of young men and women are trying to find their way through a bewildering array of new expectations. They are moving step by step through school to a decent job and marriage. The industrious youngster is often working in an atmosphere of violence and antisocial activity. He is struggling against a current which always threatens to envelop him. In fact, the young men and women who are doing a good job today are more to be commended than their forebears. They are resisting temptations of which their parents never dreamed. They are bombarded with movies and TV programs which depict easy success and provide easy money for a few smart answers. Everything is against them except their own integrity and the encouragement of some adult leaders and teachers. Their enjoyment of life and willingness to work should not be slighted because of the prevailing revolt of their contemporaries. Nevertheless, the revolt of youth has become a national problem. The revolt may not have extended to the majority of young men and women, but it has increased steadily over the years.

It is generally agreed that home life has something to do with the revolt of youth. Just how much the family has to do with this remains an uncertain question. Many people blame the whole problem on the family. Judges occasionally reprimand parents for their failure to discipline their youngsters properly. Several judges attempted to impose sentences on the parents rather than the children, since they felt that the legal responsibility for juvenile crime lay with the parents. On the other hand, many parents blame the companions with whom their children associate. "Johnny was a good boy until he started going around with that bunch on the corner." Other parents blame comics, movies, TV programs, and newspaper stories. "Violence has become commonplace in the comics and on TV. This is all our children see. What can you expect?" Others have blamed lack of religion, too much moving around, lack of roots, and the access to cars. Others point to the anonymity of the asphalt jungle—one simply is not known a few blocks away. Teachers blame the parents. Parents blame the gang. Each group looks to the other to solve the problems. The storekeeper looks to the police. The police look to teachers and parents.

We cannot enter into the full scope of the problem presented by the revolt of youth. This problem touches a whole range of questions from urban planning and housing to legal and correctional practices. Our concern is not with extreme cases but with the average family's share in the creation and solution of the problem. Despite much popular opinion, we cannot attribute the whole responsibility to the parents. Nevertheless, the parents do share the responsibility and can do some things to help their children through the years of transition.

Parents carry responsibility for a child's development in two principal ways. They give him direction and character as they deal with him at home. They also guide him as they share with the agencies which train him in the years of transition. Since there is an abundance of excellent material on parental responsibility within the home, we can treat this matter with some brevity. Parents are being deluged with literature on baby care, discipline, and teen-age rights. It may be useful, however, to relate these issues to the struggle for personal intimacy within the home. On the other hand, parental participation in school, church, and neighborhood activities is still a rather confused issue. Some parents are swamped with duties in Scout programs, Sunday schools, Parent-Teacher Associations, and other programs for the young. Other parents never share in the work of these agencies and institutions. Many parents feel that these groups have taken over too many parental responsibilities. They resent the intrusion of school activities on their parental obligations. Others would like to have the school take their children for twenty-four hours of the day. The tie between parents and the transitional groups in which their children share has yet to be worked out clearly in our time. We shall give more careful consideration to this aspect of parental responsibility.

Children within the Home

William H. Whyte, Jr., in describing the inhabitants of Park Forest, Illinois, uses a very perceptive illustration. In his book, *Organization Man*, he cites a nursery advertisement which describes the method of transplanting bushes. The bushes are transplanted year after year, so that their roots are numerous and short. This process makes the bushes easy to transplant with a minimum of risk. They have no deep roots which would be severed as they were moved. Mr. Whyte suggests that this is also true of organization man who must be on the move. He must put down many roots, but he cannot risk planting roots which are too deep.

This illustration pertains even more to children today than it does to organization man. Children are in transition from the time that they enter school. They move slowly from the intimate circle of the family through friendships, school, part-time employment and jobs into an independent existence. Their roots in the family can give them a start for this period of transition, but they are destined to live their own lives outside this family orbit. The story told about an Episcopal bishop in New England is applicable here. A Chicago firm had asked him for a recommendation concerning a young man whom they were considering for employment. The bishop gave a lengthy account of the young man's family background. The firm is reputed to have replied that they were not considering the young man for breeding purposes. The bishop, of course, quite rightly viewed a man's family background as a good indication of the kind of character one might expect. On the other hand, companies are interested in a man's reliability and skill. Within reasonable limits, every young man must make his way on the basis of his own character and ability. He must work out his life independently of his family. His years of transition prepare him for this independence. If he is too deeply rooted in the intimacy of the family, he cannot make the transition.

If we accept the fact that children must go through the transition to an independent life, we realize that they need roots which can take hold in any soil. The roots of personal life are the relationships which persons have with one another. For example, a child may never be allowed to make his own decisions. He may grow up in an atmosphere where his parents either decide for him or subtly manipulate him into doing what they want. He never learns to take responsibility for his decisions and actions. He does not learn to allocate his own money or buy his clothes. He thinks that he is making up his own mind only to see in retrospect that his parents jockeyed him into their way of thinking. His life has been rooted deeply in dependence upon his parents. They know what is right. He knows nothing. As this child matures and moves into other groups, he will either look back to his parents for guidance or find some other adult on whom he can lean. He will not take responsibility for his own life. He will never achieve independence. He has not been given roots which can take hold in any new soil, because he is merely carrying his relation to his parents into every new situation and transforming his associates into substitute parents.

There are two kinds of roots in the family which can take hold in new soil. A family can give a child some feeling of personal integrity and responsibility. Parents can also ground a child's life in a religious faith which extends beyond the narrow confines of the home. Unbelievers would claim that personal integrity can develop in a child without religious faith. Whether this is true or not, a believer would say that these two roots are inseparable. Consequently we shall treat personal integrity and religious faith as intertwined in a child's development. A child's experiences with parents, brothers and sisters develop attitudes and convictions which he will carry all through his life. These attitudes will undergo transformations with each new experience, but their fundamental character will persist. He may see himself as a responsible person with a right to exist, or he may see himself as a nobody who always has to apologize for being alive. He may see his parents as godlike figures who must always be right, or he may see them as fallible human beings who struggled to protect and nurture him according to their abilities and insights. Religious faith is significant to this sense of personal integrity, since it sets the parents under a higher authority to which they also are subject. On the other hand, parents may use religious faith simply as a means to reinforce their own whimsical desires—threatening the child with everlasting punishments as a means of controlling him. In any case, the sense of being an acceptable person and the anchorage of life in values beyond family, gang, or school are roots which a child can plant in every new relationship and group through which he passes.

It is difficult for parents to give a child a sense of personal integrity if they are overly anxious about success. Anxiety about success leads us to impose our dreams of success on children. If we are afraid of our own failures, we become fearful of any inadequacy in our children. We hold a yardstick to our children and mete out affection for achievements. In fact, the more inadequate a father feels in his job, the more he will look to his children for the successes which he has missed. Mothers have also been caught in this dream of success. As they

have been cut off from any avenue through which to
pursue a "successful" career, they will tend to hold the
yardstick to the children even more rigidly than the fathers. Their children can live out the success from which
they have been barred. The girls can achieve the romantic success which mother missed. We see this in the pressure from mothers to get their sixth- and seventh-grade
girls into formal dresses for dances even before the children have heterosexual interests. We see it in the maternal pressure for boys to be bigger, stronger, smarter,
or more popular than Johnny down the street. This
"yardstick" rearing shrivels a youngster and destroys his
sense of integrity. He comes to feel that he is only an acceptable person so long as he is adequate. The fact of
human life is that all of us are adequate only to degrees
and in certain settings. None of us is completely adequate. Such pressure to be adequate merely makes us
anxious and dependent on any group which will accept
us. The deep root of personal integrity is shaken by expectations arising from the frustrations and inadequacies of parents.

Parents have many opportunities to break this vicious
circle which is created by the concern for success. We
make mistakes in disciplining our children. We are neither infallible nor perfect. We punish trivial things with
severity because we are tired or worried. We let serious
infractions go unpunished. We tell Johnny to stay in his
room for an hour. His sister has been busy coloring, but
now Johnny torments her through the door. The little
sister begins to cry and fuss. Soon Johnny is out on the
street, free of the discipline. Johnny begins to wonder
whether we mean what we say. He begins to see discipline as a whimsical matter which fluctuates with his
parents' moods. Children perceive favoritism and errors
in justice. They often throw these things up to their parents in confidential moments or in the heat of argument.

If parents are anxious about their own adequacy, they may be defensive about their errors in judgment and fits of temper. They may make Johnny feel that he is wrong in questioning this reign of whimsical justice. On the other hand, parents can admit their mistakes to their children. The child develops trust in his own judgment through such realistic confession. He knows in his heart that the parent has dealt unjustly with him. This insight needs the confirmation of the parent.

It seems a trivial thing to admit mistakes to children. All of us like to think that we are capable of doing it. Nevertheless, we live in a society which encourages us to pretend that we are right. Put up a good front! Don't show your weaknesses! Play your long suit! Such pretended adequacy can permeate all of a person's life. It pervades the atmosphere of the home. Some years ago a football coach took some of his team to task for shaking their heads and snapping their fingers when they missed a pass. He called them crap shooters. His point was very simple. Don't shake your heads and snap your fingers as though something happened to make you miss the pass. Don't pretend that you really would have caught the pass unless something had happened. You missed the pass! Don't miss the next one! Now we have the word "goof" on the American scene. No one makes a mistake. He "goofs." Somehow it is all right to "goof," but be sure you do not admit to making a mistake. Parents start a child on the way to an honest appraisal of himself by being realistic about their own mistakes. They also confirm a child's sense of his capacity to judge the merits of a situation. He may begin to realize that he is going to make mistakes and need not pretend to an adequacy which he does not possess. At the same time he will be confirmed in his conviction of the adequacy of his judgment in certain situations.

These parental injustices to children are also occasions for confession and forgiveness in a family. We parents are sometimes very cruel to children in the heat of our impatience. We punish them too severely or we cut them with a harsh, inexcusable sarcasm. A child is usually ready to forgive such cruelty after the initial hurt is over. In fact, children often recover from the hurt more readily than parents recover from their own feelings of guilt over what they have done. Parents can build a whole new dimension of life for children by confessing their injustices and asking forgiveness. These experiences help a child to see that forgiveness is part of the fabric of every human relationship. We often pass these things over and hope that they will be forgotten. We hate to face our own feelings of guilt over them and would prefer to let the matter be forgotten. In avoiding the issue, however, we deprive the child of a fundamental religious experience.

The experience of forgiveness works in all the relationships of a family. It can operate between brothers and sisters. Children can experience the forgiveness of their parents for their own misdeeds. They can face their envy and jealousy of an older brother or sister. However, children should not always be on the receiving side of forgiveness. They are not always in the wrong and their personal integrity is shaken when parents use forgiveness in order to strengthen the parental rightness. Children also need the opportunity to forgive the godlike figures who mete out justice and money. This experience sets the rightness of things above the whims of parents. Children learn that parents are also subject to a rightness which they cannot determine. They also learn that transgression of this rightness is not the end of a relationship. In fact, they learn that transgressions can be the opportunities for deeper personal relationship.

It is necessary to stress the importance of confession and forgiveness in a day when all of us are encouraged to pretend that we are adequate. However, children also need to have confidence in their parents' judgment and capacity. This confidence should be built on real foundations and not pretense, but it should be the normal climate of a home. Bruno Bettelheim's work with disturbed children has amply demonstrated the importance of childlike confidence in parental care. His book, *Love Is Not Enough,* recounts many instances in which a child's lack of confidence in his parents had shattered his inner security. In stressing the importance of confession and forgiveness, we need to bear in mind the importance of this normal climate of the home. Parents strengthen a child's confidence by providing him with reasonable care and decent surroundings. Many parents cannot provide as adequately for their children as they might wish, but most parents can meet a child's basic needs on a continuing and stable basis. Parents cannot escape certain aspects of the godlike role of provider of all things necessary and good. Children need parents who are capable of managing the affairs of daily life.

The child's need for confidence points up the fallacy in so much of the supposed democracy in the modern family. Mothers dress and act like sisters to their daughters. Fathers act like friends rather than fathers. Children are consulted on every issue, even matters which are far beyond their emotional maturity. Worries about money are discussed openly before very young children who cannot see these matters in a total perspective. The parent-child relationship gives way to a pseudodemocratic process in which all members of the family are treated as equals.

There is obviously real merit in developing democratic procedures within the home. Since children must develop a capacity to make decisions and use their own judgment, they need opportunities to take responsibility according to their years. Teen-agers should not have to produce a bill of rights in order to obtain a reasonable voice within the family. On the other hand, parents cannot renounce their responsibility for the direction of family affairs. They have no right to impose their financial anxieties on children before the children are mature enough to gain some perspective on these questions. We have already discussed the rule of children which arises as parents give up their responsibility for the direction of the family. Parents owe it to their children to set clear policies in matters of discipline and to maintain these policies with reasonable exceptions. They also need to decide a multitude of questions which children will not be able to face until they are older. The idea of one person, one vote, simply does not apply to family life. The relations between parents and children are by nature unequal relations, even though they are always in the process of becoming equal as the children mature. A child's confidence in his world and his capacity to manage his own affairs can be shattered by the expectation that he participate as an equal with his parents. Parents may look to children for guidance on family policies with the purpose of developing a sense of responsibility in the children. If the children are young, the parents may simply shatter the child's confidence in the world around him.

It is almost a cliché to say that children need acceptance in the modern home. Nevertheless, this cliché cannot be repeated too often under the pressures of our way of life. Parents have as much difficulty accepting their children's inadequacies as they do accepting one another. These inadequacies are too upsetting. Fathers are often crushed to discover that their boys are not popular and successful athletes. This is important to men in our time. These are symbols of success in the teens and tokens of future success. But the child is who he is. He is in part the creation of his parents. He will have to live as who he is. He can change, but only as he is accepted for the person he really is. If he does not receive this acceptance from his parents, he will never be able to accept himself. He will strive throughout life to be acceptable to others on their terms. He will never risk his security with others by being himself. He will look desperately to marriage for an acceptance which he cannot bestow upon himself. Alternatively, he may never sustain an intimate relationship or participate creatively with others. He may simply withdraw into an isolated and anxious world, needing others and yet resenting them.

This problem of acceptance is even more difficult for mothers in our day. They have too big an investment in their children's success. This investment increases with the frustration of their own ambitions, but it is also aggravated by their husbands' failures. If a woman feels she may not have a ranch house, she can hope that her children will have it. Under these pressures, acceptance comes to children as a rare gift.

Children can experience acceptance as parents listen to them and discover who these children really are. It can be experienced as parents stand with their children while the youngsters explore their own real interests and possibilities. This does not mean that children should be allowed to follow their own paths without regard to responsibilities in school and community. There are certain skills which children must learn if they are to survive in our society. However, every child will have his own style in meeting these expectations. One will be successful and in the center of every group. Another may seek isolation in his own pursuits. Children cannot live out their parents' failures without losing their own integrity. They cannot cope with the years of transition unless they can follow their own style of life. If they cannot be who they really are within the home, they can never be themselves in life. Acceptance creates the root of integrity which will continue with children through the years of transition. As they discover this acceptance within the home, they discover the fundamental acceptance by God on which all personal life is grounded. We allow others to be who they are, as we discover that God loves us as we are. God first loves us and then leads us into the kind of life which he intends for us. This is the pattern of love through which parents can lead children to the fulfillment of their possibilities. The process simply cannot work in reverse without crippling a child's integrity. Acceptance must precede growth.

The need for affection in the modern home is another difficulty in the intimate family. Children are expected to give too much affection to their parents, and consequently they are shackled to their parents. They are bound to the family as though they were expected to stay within it for life. Thus, parents create a taproot in the family which must be severed at some point in transition. The severing of this root has serious consequences for the child and the parents.

We have already described the flight from intimacy in modern marriage. One consequence of this flight is that mother, father, or both look for intimacy with their children which they cannot find in the marriage. This is an impossible demand to place on children, since youngsters are not mature enough to give this affection to parents. It is, moreover, a distorted demand, since the parents are not married to the children. The children must ultimately move out of the family to their own lives. Where parents create such excessive needs for affection in their children by possessing them, the children must turn against the parents in order to gain freedom. They may turn away by rejecting the expectations of school and society. They may resort to violence in order to hide from themselves their own need for their parents. They may simply fail in school. On the other hand, they may be too good in school and develop into "prissy" people who have to hide their resentments by pretending to themselves and others that they are really kind and responsible. In either case a child cannot gain a sense of personal integrity if his parents have possessed him in every breath and action.

Parents are not necessarily falsifying when they stand up in court after a child's delinquency and say that their son was a good boy. The boy may well have accommodated himself to his parents. He may have eaten all the health-giving food that his mother stuffed into his mouth. He may have kept his clothes clean to please mother. He may have reported all his doings to his ever watchful supervisor. Finally he revolted along the only path open to him. He never had privacy. He was never allowed to be himself. Everything sociable and useful was tied up with this all-consuming possession by his mother. Violence and antisocial activities were the only path to freedom and privacy. His escape from his parents led him to violent acts. Secretly he revenged himself against his parents. He was a good boy. In fact, he was merely the object of parental frustration.

Such rebellions are relatively unusual, although they are occurring in increasing numbers. The usual form of rebellion against excessive affection in the home is through a break with the parents. This begins in the teen-age period with surliness and irresponsibility. It leads in time to a clean break with the family. Since the child has been given too little privacy and independent life, he must decide for himself or for his parents. Society presses him to decide for himself. His own interests lead him to seek freedom and the opportunity to be himself. If he has been made too dependent, he cannot make the break. He spends the rest of his life looking after his parents and trying to meet their excessive demands for attention. He gives up his girls one after another, since

no girl is suitable to the parents. On the other hand, he
may still have enough independence to lead his own
life, but he lacks the personal integrity to keep a relationship with his parents while pursuing his own interests. Consequently he must break all relations with his
parents. He seldom sees them again. When he does see
them, it is usually unsatisfying all around and leads to
recriminations for inattention or hurt feelings over trivial slights.

It is no easy matter to give a child personal integrity
and sound convictions within the intimacy of the modern home. We are always drawing him too closely into
the circle of intimacy or pressing him too hard to be
independent and self-reliant. We look for too much or
too little. We press him to succeed in sports and overlook his failures in school. We push him to do well in
school and forget that he needs time for friends and
recreation. Even the suggestions made above, which are
after all merely a distillation of a few generally accepted
principles, have to be applied differently with every
child. The uniqueness of each child is the personal quality in human life. We cannot distill formulae which will
work with all children. Every parent knows that he or
she is adjusting certain policies in accordance with the
needs of the particular child. One needs more discipline.
Another needs less pressure and more warmth. And so it
goes.

In view of the difficulties of this parental task, one
word of caution should be said about this discussion of
children within the home. Every new book on child-rearing is adding to parental feelings of guilt. We followed
too rigid a schedule or we did not schedule life enough.
We argued in front of children or we never let the child
see any of our emotions. We realize that we have made
mistakes with our children, however well intended those
mistakes may have been. If we have made really serious

mistakes which grew out of the distortions of our own personalities, we owe it to the child to provide opportunities for therapy and guidance. Such guidance is available through clinics and guidance centers for families in all income brackets. Most of us, however, have made less serious mistakes. We have passed on many anxieties, but the child is quite capable of managing as well or better than his parents. If this be the case, we do well to remember that the book is not closed after six, ten, or sixteen years of age. A child has his own life to lead and he will grow and change through many experiences. We merely perpetuate our desires to possess our children by imagining that we are the sole creators of their lives.

We parents do well to recall the story of Joseph and his brothers when we are plagued with feelings of guilt about mistakes that we have made with our children. Joseph's envious brothers had sold him into slavery. Joseph finally rose to a position of prominence in Pharaoh's house. Meanwhile, drought and famine spread through the whole land and Joseph's brothers came into Egypt to purchase grain. Joseph disclosed his identity to his brothers with the following words:

> So Joseph said to his brothers, "Come near to me, I pray you." And they came near. And he said, "I am your brother, Joseph, whom you sold into Egypt. And now do not be distressed, or angry with yourselves, because you sold me here; for God sent me before you to preserve life. For the famine has been in the land these two years; and there are yet five years in which there will be neither plowing nor harvest. And God sent me before you to preserve for you a remnant on earth, and to keep alive for you many survivors. So it was not you who sent me here, but God . . ."

GENESIS 45:4–8

This story cannot be used to free us from responsibility for our transgressions against our children. However, the story sets human actions in their proper perspective. God uses our actions to accomplish His purposes. Our actions are always inadequate and imperfect to a degree. We never love enough or care enough. We are seldom honest enough in the appraisal of a situation. Nevertheless, God uses our attempts to minister to children in order to bring those children to the life which He intends. We can well afford an honest acknowledgment of our faults in child-rearing. These are matters for which we need forgiveness. On the other hand, we have no right to arrogate to ourselves the role of God with our children. They must lead their own lives and ultimately they must answer to God for the way in which they have used what little we could give them.

School, Church, and Neighborhood

Parents fulfill part of their responsibility in the home. Family experience lays the groundwork for personal integrity and religious conviction, but a child must pass through many other groups before achieving maturity. He will be subject to the pressures of his friends or gang. He must sort out their values and accommodate himself through compromise or withdrawal. He must make some kind of adjustment to the expectations of his teachers. His church will demand loyalty. These demands may fit with his family background or thrust him into serious conflicts with his parents. With each step along the way, he is encountering new demands for loyalty and new responsibilities. Parents cannot fulfill their responsibilities to children by watching this process as spectators. Parents have too big a stake in the development of their children to stand by while others guide them. On the other hand, parents cannot take over the tasks of friends, school, and church, since these groups serve to free the children from too much dependency on their parents. Parents have to share in this process of transition without dominating it.

This is a familiar problem to all parents. How much should they tamper with their children's selection of friends? Should they encourage certain friends and guide their children away from others? How much should they participate in church, scout, and neighborhood activities with their children? The parents are busy. They are pressed with their own concerns. The children are caught up in a dozen different groups. How can the parents distribute their time among these groups without being pulled out of the home into a multiplicity of activities?

The division of time among different groups is not the only problem for parents in participating with their children. The transitional process is a relatively new thing. Parents are not always clear where their responsibility begins and ends. Should the churches give all the religious instruction or is this primarily a parental responsibility? How much responsibility should parents carry for the education of their children? Is this entirely a job for the schools or is it partly a parental task? If parents are to share in the educational process, how is this to be done? Should they work with the teachers through associations, or primarily by supplementing the work of the schools? Should mother and father merely see that Johnny does his homework or should they take some real part in the direction of school life? The answers to these questions are not clear-cut today, since neither teachers nor parents are certain of the division of responsibility. The churches are likewise unclear as to how much responsibility they should carry for Christian education. They are looking for parental help, but they are not at all certain of the realistic distribution of these responsibilities. Should parents merely set an example by going to church themselves or should they also do the actual instruction of the children?

The division of responsibility is particularly confusing with respect to the neighborhood gang and friends. Should parents set the standards for hours, activities, and recreation for these groups? If so, how can parents exercise this responsibility without cooperation from other parents in the neighborhood? Some parents are strict. Others are lenient. If the parents cannot agree, their children are caught in conflicting loyalties. This is partly a question of uncertainty about responsibility and partly a result of the fact that most families are isolated from one another in the neighborhoods. Parents rarely discuss such matters, since they have no natural communities in which to share their common concerns. The intimate privacy of the modern family militates against such neighborhood cooperation, and this social vacuum in the neighborhood leaves the door open for young people to set their own standards of behavior. Since the young are often rebelling against adult demands, these standards of behavior may range all the way from irresponsibility to war on the society.

There are three major groupings with which the modern family can be closely allied in the guidance of their children. Two of these groups already exist and desire the cooperation of parents—the school and the church. The coalitions of family with the school and family with church are natural alliances, but the division of responsibility is far from clear. The third grouping is the neighborhood. This group exists only in informal ways in most urban areas. The development of teen-age problems indicates that the neighborhood group may prove to be the most fundamental alliance for the family. In fact, the alliances with school and church cannot be visualized apart from a real development of a community of parents by neighborhoods.

The *school* is one of the most crucial groups in the transitional years. Parents are already allied to the schools through school boards and Parent-Teacher Associations. In most cases these have not been very successful alliances, since there is usually an undercurrent of mistrust between teachers and parents. Nevertheless, the relationship between teachers and parents is the focal point of cooperation. The family must be allied to the school if parents are to fulfill their responsibilities.

Parents are suspicious of teachers for many reasons. The most obvious reason is the fact that teachers are replacing the parents as guides for their children. After reaching third or fourth grade, the children are obeying the teachers and questioning the authority of the parents. They are contradicting their parents with the latest view on pronunciation or current events. High-school girls come home with instructions on table-setting or cooking which do not suit mother. Boys have learned that many of the things which father believes are no longer true. Children are caught between competing authorities and they naturally fall toward the one which frees them from parental control.

The inherent conflict between parent and teacher also has its roots in the American philosophy of "my children." Other children may be unruly or disobedient, but *my* children are perfect. Johnny-down-the-street may need punishment in school, but my child would get along fine if he had a decent teacher. No teacher is going to lay hands on *my* child. If the school system were good, *my* Jane would know how to read. The philosophy is *my* family first, last, and always. Everyone on the street is wrong except my children. One may think this is an exaggerated picture but just try suggesting to a parent that he is handling his children badly. Parents who have tried this know that it is the surest way to end a friendship. This philosophy works against parent-teacher cooperation. The teacher needs the help of the parents in understanding the children and in strengthening her hand with the children. The parents need the teacher's insight about the children, since he or she sees the child in a new light. Nevertheless, the teacher is hesitant to offend the parents, and the parents are unwilling to listen to the teacher. Parents automatically assume that the teacher is wrong and Johnny is right. The teacher is guilty until proved innocent.

The mistrust is not only on the parents' side. Teachers have also contributed to this conflict. Public-school teachers have been notoriously underpaid and insecure in their positions. This has been somewhat less true in large cities with pension systems and unions, but it is still generally true. This job insecurity has been increased by the purges and red-baiting of recent years. The schools should be free to open minds to new ideas, but teachers feel pressed to tread the safest possible ground. They have felt, with some justice, that they must remain above criticism at all points, including their private lives. Such an atmosphere breeds suspicion and mistrust. It has been difficult for teachers to overcome this atmosphere and deal frankly with parents. They find themselves operating tactfully with parents and expecting the worst. Such a climate does not lead to frank communication.

The occupational insecurity of teachers has also led to a drive for status in the teaching profession. This is perfectly natural in any occupation which feels underpaid in terms of its contribution to society and the years of training required for its practice. The net result, however, has been the professionalization of teaching. Teachers are working with their own technical vocabulary and assuming that parents will not understand them. Teachers are now pushed to work for advanced degrees in order to gain promotions. These degrees may be helpful in their teaching, but they usually represent more time spent in courses than real development as teachers. This is primarily a phase of the drive for status. The consequence of all this is a widening gap between parents and teachers. Many teachers have simply given up the attempt to share their concerns with parents "who wouldn't understand anyway."

The conflict between parents and teachers has also grown around uncertainty in spheres of responsibility. Teachers have inherited many of the family's functions in teaching manners, sociability, and hygiene. Schools have taken over much of the social and recreational life of children. Some schools even plan week-end trips for children. Many of these activities fall into an uncertainty area between family and school responsibility. Parents feel that they should have more voice in the kinds of social activities in which their children are expected to participate. Should the school plan a formal party for high-school freshmen? Should the children be lured into school activities when the family has planned its own outing? This uncertainty about responsibility can only be clarified through cooperation between teachers and parents. Since there is very little communication, the mutual mistrust is deepened and the spheres of responsibility are never clarified.

These are not new problems. Every parent has wrestled with them through the years. They are problems created by a new way of life and a new system for training children. We sometimes forget that the public-education system is a rather recent development. The implications of public education are just now being felt, and parents are faced with the responsibility of taking some part in the process or standing helplessly on the sidelines. It is perfectly clear that parents will have no hand in the process if they continue to act with suspicion toward the teachers. Such mistrust leads the teachers further into professional secrecy and tactful evasion. On the other hand, teachers will continue to be plagued with problems of discipline if they cannot elicit parental help.

Alliances between parents and teachers have been experimented with in a great many schools. Teachers, school administrators, and parents have become increasingly concerned with the question. The line of constructive development is still far from clear, but a few clues have emerged. If we assume that parents and teachers are willing to minimize their mutual suspicions in order to achieve a reasonable level of cooperation, we can detect certain possibilities.

— It is quite evident that married women with proper training should be encouraged to do part-time or full-time teaching. This is not meant as a slur on the excellent work done by single teachers. It is simply an advantage to have a certain number of parents in the teaching field who can mediate between the single teachers and the parents. Married teachers often see both sides of the problem with more objectivity and are somewhat more secure in their position within the community. This applies even more to married men. Most teaching jobs cannot pay a married man adequately, and consequently our children are too much under the tutelage of women. If we can count on an increase in leisure time in the coming years, and there is every reason to assume this, then men should be given more encouragement to do part-time teaching. Although this may sound like a prejudiced remark, it seems reasonable to hope for more objectivity from men in the task of cooperation between teachers and parents.

One further clue seems reasonably clear. Parents should share in the planning of all activities in school which do not pertain directly to academic learning. In fact, social and recreational activities should be the full responsibility of parents with the cooperation of a few teachers. These activities are not the responsibility of the teachers, and yet there is good reason to encourage such events within school life. Social and recreational activities help to weld children together in a school. This is particularly true in schools of different ethnic and racial composition. Such activities also provide a natural expression for the children's sense of belonging to the school community. Teachers have often organized these activities under pressure from the youngsters. The need has been evident. Since parents defaulted, teachers stepped in. Most teachers are too overworked to assume this responsibility and need parental cooperation. Moreover, this is a crucial sphere in which parents can relate their family values to the natural community in which their children are participating.

This is not a new idea. Some schools have developed parental participation to a marked degree. It is emphasized here because it is the logical point for practical cooperation between parents and teachers. Experiences in practical cooperation provide the ground for understanding and mutual confidence. Nevertheless, cooperation in planning recreational activities is no easy matter. Many parents do not want to be bothered with school problems. They are glad to have the teachers take the children off their hands. This is what they pay for, is it not? Why should parents do the teachers' job? On the other hand, teachers sometimes dislike the activities that parents want. Teachers are often more conservative about children's activities than parents. It is hard enough to run a school without having a lot of meddling parents underfoot. And tensions arise when parents from different economic and ethnic groups begin to plan recreational activities. Differences in style of life come to the surface. Such conflicts make school administrators feel that they have enough problems without adding parental prejudices. These are a few of the difficulties which ensue when parents begin to participate in school life. Nevertheless, such practical cooperation in a sphere of mutual concern—the building of a common life among the children of a school—is a logical point for parent-teacher cooperation.

The Parent-Teacher Associations provide a natural vehicle for this cooperation. These associations have usually bogged down in fund-raising for bands or other special projects instead of pursuing their real business. These projects have been substitute activities which divert parents from their central concerns with school life. They have also fitted the American pattern of doing something to appear constructive. The P.-T.A. has usually proved unsatisfying to parents and teachers. It is, nevertheless, a fundamentally sound vehicle, if it can address its attention to the real problems. The development of the social life of the school is merely one among many areas of parent-teacher cooperation which the P.-T.A. could foster.

We have no basis for predicting the degree of mutual confidence which may emerge from practical cooperation. Mistrust between parents and teachers is built into our way of life. Teachers seem to be the scapegoats for parental failures with their children. It is obvious that parents can appreciate the teacher's position more adequately through participation in the organization of the school community. Such appreciation many lead to more willingness to take counsel with teachers on the handling of children. It could lead to more support for the teaching job in the home. These are merely hopes, but they represent great gains over the spectator role of parents.

The *church* is, of course, a long-standing ally of family

life. This alliance has a special character, however, so far as it pertains to the development of children. Sunday schools and youth programs in churches have provided transitional loyalties for children. In fact, the Sunday school has often been the means for bringing adults to the church. Mary gets to be four or five and notices that her playmates are going to Sunday school. She visits the church with a friend. Soon she has joined the Sunday school and the minister calls at home. Within a few months, the whole family may be going to church. Parents seem to follow the interests of children and even make their acquaintances through their children. Church membership has varied with Sunday school programs. This is probably inevitable in a child-centered society, where families are striving to provide the best for their children.

Ministers have begun to evaluate their Sunday school and youth programs rather critically. They realize that membership pivots around a successful Sunday school, but they are not sure what they are accomplishing through this activity. Moreover, the ministers realize that they are not able to teach children without parental participation. Bible stories and moral lessons can be taught Sunday after Sunday, but the child's values, attitudes, and convictions are imparted at home. The parents may follow the child to church, but their convictions are already formed. Church membership may mean little more than attendance and financial contributions.

The evaluation of youth programs has also shaken confidence in youth activities. Young men and women have enjoyed some of their finest personal experiences in the church's camping and conference programs. Critical evaluation of Sunday school and youth activities has been forced to acknowledge this, while questioning the long-range import of the program. Sunday school religion seems to be the only religion imparted in this process. The strong meat of the Christian faith never seems to get across to the majority. Youth religion seems to be a special experience of "fellowshipping" which is sloughed off with adulthood, leaving only a slight residue of good feeling about the church.

Every evaluation of these transitional groups brings the minister back to the question of parental participation. Religious life must pervade the daily life of a family if the church is to fulfill its teaching and pastoral work with the young. The church cannot be a substitute parent. Nevertheless, the church cannot drop its work with children and young people, since it is responsible to keep contact with all age groups.

Many parents are as troubled as the ministers about the Sunday school program. Parents have sought support from the churches in the maintenance of family unity. The usual Sunday school program divided the family into age groups. Parents on the way to church met their children returning from Sunday school. Parish activities divided families by sex, age, and interest. In recent years, churches have begun to change their programs to meet family needs. Many churches now have midmorning family services which have larger congregations than the traditional adult services. Couples clubs and family activities are becoming quite common in many churches. Nevertheless, these changes have left the daily life of the household untouched.

The question is how far the church must go in meeting family needs? Can churches touch the daily life of the home without centering church activities in household and neighborhood? Family life has become a private, intimate sphere in our day. Can this sphere of intimacy be touched by programs centering in a church building?

Several experiments in bringing the church to the household indicate that the emphasis should be on neighborhood and household rather than the church building. A group of ministers in the Harlem area of New York have developed a ministry of this kind in several blocks. This is painstaking and difficult work, but it touches the daily life of people. A ministry to neighborhoods and families is soon caught up in problems of housing, hygiene, politics, employment, discrimination, and the hundred other things that make up human existence. Christianity can bring perspective, insight, and power to such questions, but only as it becomes implicated in them. This approach does not obviate the need for organized activities and programs, but it uses organization as a resource rather than a substitute for dealing with life.

Churches often become identified with the prosperous and acceptable people. The church buildings are sometimes ornate and expensive. Many less privileged people do not feel at home in this atmosphere and refuse to attend. They may let their children attend activities at the church, but they feel too far removed from such a splendid setting. Ministers have had to move into store fronts or neighborhood households in order to reach this group of people. This was part of the problem which led to the East Harlem Experiment. Some critics have said that this approach may be necessary in these areas but need not be used in other parts of the city. However, the neighborhood approach has also proved necessary in wealthier areas.

Ernest Southcott confronted a similar question some twelve years ago in Leeds, England. He was rector of a good-sized Anglican parish. Some people were attending regularly, although many parishioners never approached the church except for baptisms, marriages, and burials. The rector knew that the parish had a ministry to all the members in the area and set about discovering how this ministry could be exercised. With the help of laymen, he eventually developed a ministry to households through which the life of the church could take root. The daily celebration of Holy Communion took place in the kitchens of the households. Instruction in baptism, confirmation, and the Christian understanding of life took place in these households. Weekly services of worship and weekly meetings of the parish gathered the large fellowship at the church building. The rest of the real ministry of the parish extended into the households and neighborhoods of the community. These household groups were not exclusive gatherings of members but were held open to all neighbors and interested persons.

Ernest Southcott has told this story in his book *The Parish Comes Alive*. We need not repeat the story here. The essential point is that Holton Parish, Leeds, was unwilling to let the daily life of its families go untouched. The parish was unwilling to go through motions in the church building as a substitute for permeating the life of the people with the new life in Christ. They had no choice but to go where the people were living out their lives in family and neighborhood. Many who read this account say that we do not need such a radical approach here. It is all right for England, where people ignore the church. American people are going to church. We only have to improve what we are doing in our churches. Unfortunately this does not seem an accurate appraisal of the situation and does not tally with what we know about the Sunday school religion of the American churches.

There are many difficulties connected with religious training of children by neighborhoods. Much more time would have to be given to the training of parents. There are many organizational problems which arise when the Sunday school moves out of the parish hall. In fact, this approach assumes the existence of a fellowship of parents who are studying, discussing, and learning together.

A program for children in neighborhoods cannot precede parental cooperation. It presupposes a community of parents who can share their concerns with one another. These parents' groups can often be started by drawing families into week-end conferences or summer camps together. They can also be started simply by raising some of the questions which trouble ministers about the Sunday school program. Many parents are deeply sensitive to these questions and are concerned to develop the integrity of their families. There are urban areas where parents are indifferent to these issues. In most areas, however, parents are desperately searching for a community in which to share their concerns and work out the religious training of their children. There is too great a distance between the intimacy of the family circle and the activities of the churches to develop this type of community in the parish building. The neighborhood makes the natural common ground on which family and church can meet.

The advantages of centering Christian training in neighborhoods far outweigh the difficulties. The most obvious advantage is that churches need not encumber themselves with huge Sunday school plants which are only used for one hour a week. The exorbitant cost of building and maintaining such plants has caught many churches in a vicious circle of fund-raising and activities. Moreover, the neighborhood is the point of contact with unchurched people. If the church becomes alive in the households and neighborhoods, it has automatically established contact with the multitude to whom it wishes to minister. Intensity and enthusiasm in a parish hall or revival tent are still a far remove from the daily life of people. Until religious faith is anchored in the places where men live and carry on their work, it remains a highly individualized and generally irrelevant activity.

The ministry to teen-agers is a somewhat more difficult problem. Very few groups have been able to utilize parents in work with teen-agers. Some parents work naturally with this age, but this time of rebellion does not take easily to parental guidance. Churches may have to continue their work with teen-agers through special programs, conferences, and camps. Even these programs must be very specialized in order to deal with delinquent gangs. The experience of the ministers at Judson Memorial Church in New York with a teen-age gang indicates that a program for such a group must be very open and fully identified with the lives of the young people. This also seems to be the experience in East Harlem. Many parents have the natural gifts to identify with young people and lead them gently into constructive pursuits. It could well be that parents with these gifts could be recruited from the neighborhood fellowships in the course of years. Laymen have so few opportunities to do anything but usher or raise funds in the church that ministers rarely know the gifts of ministry which exist in their churches. Nevertheless, only carefully selected parents have thus far been able to deal constructively with the teen-age group. The neighborhood approach is no panacea for church and family. It raises many new problems and leaves some problems untouched. However, it sets the sights on the real objective—the contact between Christianity and the daily life of the home.

The *neighborhood* has already entered the discussion as a natural setting for the family in dealing with its responsibility for the young. However, the neighborhood is a much more extensive community than the numerous religious groupings which crisscross through its streets. Churches have often divided neighborhoods, simply because they represented competing loyalties in an area. Parents realize the importance of neighborhood to their children and can reduce this tension by sharing their common concerns with family life and parental responsibilities. The crucial place of neighborhood in urban life is very evident when we consider the difficulties of supervising children in the modern city.

Those who criticize parents for juvenile delinquencies forget that parental supervision is almost impossible in the city. A sense of community is emerging in some urban neighborhoods, but many urban parents are not even acquainted with the parents of their children's playmates. The children move around more and more freely as they reach adolescence. Fathers do not work in the neighborhood, and consequently the heavy burden of supervision falls on the mother. She may not hear for weeks that her son has been running with a gang, stealing in shops, or "playfully" spilling cans of rubbish. Unless there is a common life and a network of communication in the neighborhood, the task of parental supervision is almost impossible. Children have only to roam for a few blocks to become "that kid" whom no one can identify.

Parents have brought this problem down on their own heads. In the overly intimate family, we come to resent any interference in the rearing of our children. We do not listen to the teacher's criticisms. We do not listen to the criticisms of people on the block. We do not discuss our methods for handling children with others. We operate alone. These are *our children*. But are they? These children are first of all themselves. They are also members of our family. They are also members of a community. If we are members of a church, then the children are the responsibility of the whole congregation.

The result of this parental possessiveness is that our children do not recognize the authority of other adults. This is a peculiarly modern phenomenon in human society. We live in neighborhoods where we are known only to a few people. Our children do not know many other adults, and they do not feel known. Furthermore, in those blocks where children are known, they feel no obligation to obey the words of other adults. They know that their parents will defend them against the neighbor's criticisms. Finally, our acquaintances hesitate to criticize our children, because they have lost too many friends by well-intended suggestions. Consequently the parents are being asked to do an impossible job. The moment the child is out of sight, he is free of any supervision until he is in school. We have isolated ourselves from any help in parental supervision. We have exposed our children to the whims of any group to which they become attached.

There is a further complication in this problem of parental supervision. Since parents are not sharing their ideas of what is to be expected of children, they have few common standards for children's activities. Some children are up late and free to roam beyond the immediate neighborhood. Others are kept close at hand. Some come directly home from school. Others play from block to block. Parents may have standards within the home, but children end up setting their own standards in their gangs. Some of this is inevitable. Nevertheless, parents have as much need for joining forces as their children. We spoke earlier of the rule of children in the home. We also have a rule of youngsters on the street. They set their own standards and determine their own codes of conduct. Since the parents do not come together as parents and as citizens of a community, the children take over the organization of life on the streets. No adult group is really involved in what they are doing. They have taken the rule over their lives because the adults have defaulted.

In the course of history, the churches have been primarily concerned with directing and renewing the life of already existing communities. This was a proper role, since family ties and local loyalties formed a fabric which could be penetrated with a message of God's forgiveness and righteousness. However, there is no longer a fabric of community to penetrate. There is a loose network of relationships centering around broad interests, but there is little that could be described as community in residential areas. The churches cannot assume an existing community to be penetrated and shaped. They face the task of joining with others in the creation of a new type of community which will fit urban life.

We face a peculiarly difficult problem in gaining the support of churches for the building of neighborhood community. The churches partition people into separate and often hostile groups. Each group tries to build its own loyalties, and in building these loyalties it thrusts the others out of its life. Our religious groupings often nurture sound values, but they also divide neighborhoods. Roman Catholics mistrust Protestants, and Protestants misunderstand Roman Catholics. Both groups are uncertain about the Jews, and mutual trust is broken. We shall not see the dissolution of these barriers in our lifetime, if one can judge by the present rate of development.

A fellowship of parents in a particular neighborhood cannot operate exclusively. Parents from other churches and no church at all have a similar stake in the neighborhood. Their children are on the streets. Their youngsters need guidance and supervision. It is inevitable that some group of parents must make the beginning. They must meet, talk together, study their problems and share their concerns. It is hopeless to wait until everyone is ready to enter such a project. Nevertheless, an open group can be maintained to which all comers are welcome. They can gear their discussions and plans in such a way that all interested parents are included. The problems of child-rearing and family life are common concerns of the neighborhood. They need exclude no group or individual. Single people in neighborhoods can often contribute as much as parents. These individuals also have a place in such fellowships. Personal religious convictions need not be compromised by such openness. The real issue is whether we are interested in promoting a religious organization or expressing a Christian life. Christian life is what happens on the street corner, how Johnny's delinquencies are handled, at what hour children can safely roam the streets, and how George's father can feed his family after being laid off the job. These are the problems of neighborhood and family life.

The family has been freed of many of its traditional functions by our way of life. It no longer determines the careers, marriages, prestige, and political positions of its members. Thus, the family has been freed to serve as a center of intimacy and personal companionship. This is the potential strength of the modern family. It can be a truly personal community. This concern for intimacy in the family, however, has led to isolationism. We want privacy. We want freedom to pick our friends. We want to be left alone. Let the school do its job and we shall do ours. Let the church teach the young and we shall make our contributions. Let no one interfere with the way we raise our children in the home. This is my family. These are my children. Such isolationism, however, leads to an overly intimate home. It concentrates too much attention on too few relationships. Moreover, isolationism thrusts growing children into a no-man's land of conflicting values and loyalties. Ultimately the isolationist family is irresponsible toward its youth in transition.

The modern family can legitimately claim a degree of privacy and a measure of freedom in determining its life. Parents accept a God-given responsibility when they marry and have children. They pledge loyalty to one another. They promise to raise their children in accordance with the will of God. Parents have every right to guard these responsibilities with a jealous vigilance. Ultimately they must answer to God for their faithfulness in the discharge of these duties. No school, church, or neighborhood can be allowed to pre-empt these duties from the parents. We live in a time of insecurity when people are inclined to huddle together for security. In such times, parents may be inclined to resign themselves to such collective direction. Against such pressures, family isolationism is not only commendable but necessary. This, however, is quite a different thing from cooperation between parents and teachers, parents and church groups, and parents with parents by neighborhoods. Such alliances can strengthen the integrity of the family so long as parents reserve the right to make the final decisions on all matters which affect their children. Parents cannot allow any religious or neighborhood group to determine finally the values which must be pursued in their homes. These are the prerogatives of parental responsibility. The family has its own life under God. School, church, neighborhood, and government betray their real functions when they transgress this sphere of family responsibility.

The family today, however, is not under excessive communal pressure. If anything, the family is too much isolated from the agencies which are training its children. Parents can look on teachers, religious leaders, and fellow parents as resources for their task with the children. If there are conflicts over spheres of responsibility, they need not be resolved by withdrawal. Most teachers and religious leaders are seeking reasonable cooperation from parents. Many parents in the neighborhood would cherish opportunities to work out sensible standards for the actions of the young. Such alliances can be a resource to the family rather than a threat to its integrity.

The suggestions made here for such cooperation are only tentative, since many avenues will have to be explored before adequate steps can be discerned. The problem, however, seems quite clear. The intimate family cannot fulfill its responsibility to youth in transition without new methods of participating in these transitional years. The determination of these methods, in accordance with all that has been said, must rest ultimately upon the parents.

CHAPTER SEVEN

FROM ONE GENERATION TO ANOTHER

Very few couples escape the question of what to do about a widowed parent. A young couple has established their own home. They are probably carrying a stiff mortgage and several other loans. Educational expenses are getting heavier. Then John's father dies and his mother is uncertain about her future. She has some social security money, but it is not enough to provide an adequate home. There was a little insurance, but most of the savings went for dad's illness. John feels responsible for his mother, but there is very little room for her in the house. He could let her have a little money, and yet he has little to spare. His sister is in no position to do anything about mother, since she has been having a difficult time with her husband. John's wife, Jane, is unhappy about the idea of bringing her mother-in-law into the home. They get along fine now, but what would it be like in this house twenty-four hours a day? Moreover, John's mother does not want to upset the family. Her son has had a happy marriage and she wants it to stay that way. In fact, she is not sure that she could stand the constant activity of the children. She has had some quiet years with her husband. She is not sure that her nerves can stand another experience of the comings and goings of children. On the other hand, she feels lonely and deserted. She needs company and would appreciate being with her son and his family.

In a thousand different ways, this question confronts most married couples at some point in their family life. Even grandparents who are widowed with adequate incomes feel lonely and estranged. Some want independence and a quiet place of retirement. Many want association with their children and grandchildren. Sometimes they can find this association by living in the same town or neighborhood with the children. They can stop by, do a little baby-sitting, and withdraw when things are tense. Even this solution is not always possible or satisfactory. Modern neighborhoods do not always provide accommodations for single people. Moreover, young adults are on the move and their new neighborhood may take the grandparent far from familiar surroundings. If the grandparent is not part of the family, she may find herself isolated in a strange city for long hours which are relieved only by visits with the grandchildren.

Our family life, concentrating as it does on the intimacy of parents with dependent children, has frozen out the grandparents. This development is not necessarily the result of ill will. Most young couples feel guilty about the situation. They would like to do something constructive, but they are not sure just what is constructive. We have increased the length of human life and yet made old age a period of isolation. We have improved medical knowledge and technique so that human beings live longer, but we have also made inevitable the lingering, costly illnesses of older people. It is becoming more and more expensive to die. Consequently young couples face a threat to their intimacy when they take grandparents into the home, and they also face the financial risk of costly illnesses.

Husband and wife usually start in marriage with neutrality toward the parents-in-law. The wife often has stronger ties with her mother. She may develop stronger ties with her husband's mother than he can maintain. Nevertheless, the watchword is neutrality, so that neither pair of grandparents is slighted. Christmas presents are equalized so far as possible. Visits are distributed tactfully on both sides. This, at least, is the general tendency. The attitude of neutrality and equal treatment comes back to haunt a couple when one grandparent is widowed and dependent. Why should John's mother need this special treatment? Jane's mother and father have maintained their independence. This is not fair. The neutral-but-equal doctrine has collapsed. What new principle should operate?

The question about John's mother cannot be separated from the general problem of growing old in our society. We gain perspective on this relationship by seeing the total process of aging in our society. Old age, if accompanied with reasonable health, is not after all a problem in itself. One is alive at whatever age and enjoys certain privileges and opportunities which attend a particular age in life. Sexual pleasures may diminish with age, but so do the problems of conflicting sexual loyalty. Ambition may wane, but so do the depressing conflicts of failure. Life may fall more into perspective with riper years, but this depends on the way age is understood in a particular society. Some men retire at sixty-five years and become old men overnight. Others retire at the same age and begin a new and richer life. Age itself is not the essential problem. The real question is how aging is understood. How are older people viewed by the younger generation and how do older people view themselves? Consequently the first question is what aging means today.

Growing Old in the U.S.A.

Our emphasis on productive work makes old age seem like the end of life. People have always been forced to withdraw from productive work in later years, but now they withdraw into a vacuum. In most societies, retirement from work meant entrance into the honored position of elder. One could give time to counseling the young, passing on the traditions, and sitting in the seats of the venerated. Life did not end with retirement. New life and new responsibilities followed withdrawal from hunting, fishing, war parties, or bearing children. There is no such honored position for the elder in our way of life. We honor the new, the youthful, the more efficient. Methods are changing year by year and only the most youthful can keep up with the new. Older people do get somewhat more set in their ways. This is the conserving strength of the elder in a society. He represents the wisdom of the old ways. We, on the other hand, have no place for the old ways. Even as children, we use the word old-fashioned as a term of disdain. Old age comes to mean "useless" in a society that worships the latest method and the newest invention.

We also deprive old age of its meaning by our confidence in man's control of circumstances. Despite the threat of hydrogen bombs, modern man has unlimited confidence in his ability to control his destiny. We have conquered some diseases. Give us a little more time, and we shall conquer all diseases. If oil runs short, we shall resort to atomic power. If there is strife in a factory, we can bring in the experts on human relations who will adjust all the tensions. In fact, we have to emphasize our control of the uncertainties of life in order to stimulate our pursuit of new knowledge and techniques. If this confidence flags, our efforts may diminish and the security which we seek may be jeopardized.

Older people discover that these youthful dreams are not the whole truth. Some things can be controlled, but sooner or later death approaches. Old friends are dying one at a time. George had a heart attack last year. Eleanor is ailing. The precariousness of life hits us as we grow older. Family, friends, loyalty, and religious faith take on new importance in later years. Some would cynically call this tendency of older people an attempt to find substitutes for their youthful vigor. Others would say that one can only achieve a real sense of values in our society after he has passed through the American dream of success to the realities of life. Whatever our interpretation, Americans despise the values which older people must discover if their lives are to have meaning. We are so confident of our control over life that we make older people seem senile in their sensitivity to human weaknesses.

Older people have to face some of the shabbiness of the American dream if they are to come to the faith that makes sense out of life. They have to look upon their successes and achievements in a broader perspective. Success, after all, is but one of many values in life. Older people remember the relationships which were broken by harshness. They see the importance of God's forgiveness. They live long enough to see some of the results of their good and bad deeds. Needless to say, their words about faith seem foreign to the young. This is just another sign that dad is getting old. He doesn't understand any more. He is losing touch, but it's nice that dad has found religion.

These are a few of the ways in which our way of life isolates older people. Our provisions for the aged also reflect this separation. Our medical knowledge has brought miraculous skill in perpetuating life. Men and women are kept alive in hospitals during months of ravaging disease. Drugs help, but soon they lose their effectiveness. These illnesses are costly. Many older couples spend their life's savings on these so-called "terminal" illnesses. Consequently homes for the aged are reluctant to accept older people who are not in good health. Despite these precautions, most homes for the aged are burdened with the care of bedridden patients. Many older people must be placed in nursing homes. Many others are sent to state mental hospitals which have whole sections maintained for older people. Some of these older people linger for years without a visitor or friend. They lie helplessly in bed, while overworked attendants make a vain effort to keep them clean and provide some attention.

Old-age pensions and social security have undoubtedly improved the lot of older people. Until pensions for older people can provide independence with a decent standard of living, however, we cannot deny that our provision for the aged reflects our view that they are no longer of value.

We find it difficult to face the real needs of older people because we ourselves are afraid of all that old age means. We realize that old age contradicts the values which we now cherish—youth, vigor, success, the new and the more efficient. It is difficult to see the realities of old age unless we can face the uncertainty of human life. We confess that we cannot face these facts about life by the way that we overlook the hardships of aging in our time. We know these hardships. We see them all about us. Nevertheless, we cannot really see them, because it is too disturbing to face their implications.

Even when older people can receive good accommodations and a decent standard of living, they still suffer from personal isolation. Old peoples' homes have been a boon to many, but they do not overcome the estrangement from children, younger people, and family life. The course of human life is lived in neighborhoods and homes. Daily life involves laundry, cooking, going to work, having arguments, and a hundred routine things. Older people are removed from this stream of life when they enter a home for the aged. Some of them like the quiet of such a setting and the fellowship with others of their age. Many, however, age more rapidly, become bedridden, and deteriorate under such conditions. Welfare agencies have been attempting to place older people in private homes to overcome this deterioration. Isolation from the stream of life intensifies the process of aging. One cannot escape the feeling that he is rejected by the community. Premature illness and the need for bed care become substitute ways of gaining attention. Old age becomes living death rather than a new stage of life.

New developments in our society may transform some of these conditions for older people. There is strong pressure to continue to improve pension and social security provisions. If this trend is strengthened, older people may gain a degree of independence which will place their destiny more in their own hands. We treasure our freedom to decide the circumstances of our lives, but thus far we have withheld this privilege from many older people. It remains to be seen whether we are willing to extend this privilege to them.

The shorter working week may also contribute to the freedom of older people by allowing time for outside interests during the productive years. More men and women are using their leisure time to develop avocations. Many of them, to be sure, are using leisure time to supplement their incomes with additional work, but the four-day week will undoubtedly create a serious question about the use of leisure time. Unless young adults develop creative interests, they will find TV and recreational pursuits dull and uninteresting. Leisure time is very unevenly distributed in our society, since managerial and professional people often work seven days a week, while production workers find time to carry two jobs in order to increase their incomes. Nevertheless, professional and managerial personnel usually have too many outside interests, whereas production workers have had too little energy to develop other interests. If production workers gain more leisure time and use it to develop avocations, they may well look forward to retirement from industry. In fact, the shoe may be on the other foot. Industry may be inducing workers to continue after retirement age, thus utilizing their technical skill for the problems of production. Workers, on the other hand, will have the choice of continuing in productive work or pursuing their avocations. Such a development is still in the field of working time, but it may enhance the freedom of choice for older people.

Automation is another industrial development which may benefit the older worker. Opinions differ on this subject, since the implications of automation for industrial life are still uncertain. A good case can be made, however, for the fact that automation will put a premium on technical competence and minimize youthful vigor. Most workers are quite naturally concerned over the degree of unemployment which will be created by automation. Nevertheless, automation may increase the need for technical training and thus lengthen the training period for workers. A labor scarcity is a real possibility if educational and training requirements are considerably increased. Such a development would more than offset the reduction in number of workers. This, at least, is a reasonable possibility which Peter Drucker has suggested. If this happens, the pressure to make the retirement age more flexible will be increased. Older skilled workers may be in great demand. Knowledge of complex processes is not easily gained and requires a minimum of physical strength. Older workers may have considerably more choice about their retirement in the not too distant future.

These rather optimistic considerations about old age should be countered with two rather obvious considerations. We Americans tend to live up to the limits of our income. We get a raise and think that now we shall have plenty to spare. In a few months that raise has been absorbed in a slightly higher standard of living for the family. It is hard to say just where the money went, but we have used it on a multitude of little things. There is no reason to expect that pension provisions will ever match this higher standard of living which has been achieved in the productive years. Older people have fewer expenses, since they are no longer supporting children. Nevertheless, their standard of living is bound to drop with retirement. Furthermore, American standards of thrift have changed radically since World War II. Credit buying has become standard practice. Most couples today are carrying rather heavy debts. Cars are purchased on credit. Mortgages are not new on the American scene, but many more couples are buying homes and paying on long-term mortgages. Many older people in our day have had some savings for their later years. The present generation, however, may have some equity in a house but they will have no other savings. Both of these facts, the drop in the standard of living and the lack of savings, will undoubtedly handicap our own generation as they approach retirement. These conditions may induce them to put off retirement in order to maintain their incomes. If they have greater freedom to retire or pursue avocations because of automation, they may be more inclined to continue working because of financial pressure. In any case, the financial prospects for older people look somewhat better in the years to come.

Even with increased financial independence, old age in the U.S.A. means a break with the rest of the community. Our way of life is concentrated on economic productivity and abundance. Retirement from this productive process is bound to mean alienation from the central activity of the community. Although industrial developments may extend the years of productive work, retirement from work will still mark a break with the paramount interest of our society. The question remains as to what meaning old age can have in a society which is devoted to work.

This question throws us back on the relationships of older people to their children and grandchildren. We have no venerated positions for the elders. We have little use for their wisdom, since we are more interested in the new than the old. Couples can enjoy retirement when they have companionship with one another. If they have a modicum of financial independence, these later years can be a time for relaxation. Unfortunately men work in a highly competitive situation and do not survive these later years as well as their wives. Many women do not have a period of retirement with their husbands. Their husbands die before retirement or shortly after withdrawing from the active life of work. Loneliness becomes a serious problem for the widow or widower. We cannot give them a venerated position. Can we find a place for them in the ordinary stream of family life?

Grandparents in the Home

The value of home placement for older people has been demonstrated beyond any question in the field of social welfare. Social agencies work with older people who have lost contact with their families or have no children to give them attention. Placement with a family has been beneficial in such cases. The older person enters again into the stream of life, looking after children some of the time and getting caught up in neighborhood doings. Many young families could well give thought to cooperating with social welfare agencies in this program, since it contributes to the total care of older people and exposes their children to valuable experiences with wiser and older heads. The point, however, is that life within the family is the natural place for most people, and this applies to old as well as young. Naturally the decision on such placement should rest with the older person, since it is his or her life. Nevertheless, home placement is as essential to older people as it is to those children who have become wards of the state.

There is one crucial difference between such placement and taking John's mother into the home. An older person who is placed by the welfare agency is not related to the family. She comes in as an outsider with no past history of conflicts, dependencies, and affections. She does not disrupt the neutral-but-equal relation to the parents-in-law. The family will become fond of her, and she will come to love the family. This develops slowly and naturally. John's mother, on the other hand, has special ties with John, certain inevitable jealousies of Jane, and a claim on her grandchildren. This applies to any parent-in-law whom Jane and John may feel obliged to include in their home. However, it usually applies most sharply to John's mother, as should be obvious from all that has been said in previous chapters. Any parent-in-law within the home will be to some extent a threat to the covenant of intimacy between husband and wife. The degree of threat depends on the personal maturity of the couple, the extent to which they have achieved real intimacy, and the character of the parent-in-law in question.

There seems no question that the covenant of intimacy is the prior obligation of husband and wife. This seems a harsh principle, since it may function to exclude a grandmother or grandfather who desperately needs the companionship of the home. Nevertheless, husband and wife pledge a loyalty to one another in marriage which demands that they forsake father and mother and cleave to one another. This is not said legalistically, as though this is precisely what the Bible meant by marriage. In biblical times there were obligations to parents which overrode marital obligations, including the obligation to take another wife in order to perpetuate the family name. In our society, however, the covenant of intimacy is a very personal alliance. The stability of this relationship depends on the exclusion of others from equal intimacy. The stability of personal life for parents and children rests on the fulfillment of this covenant. Neither husband nor wife has any right to set responsibility to his or her parent before this covenant of marriage. The intimacy of husband and wife with their dependent children is the prior obligation for the members. No other ties or interests can be allowed to threaten that unit. A man may have to leave his wife and children for military service in defense of his country, but this is always understood as a contribution to the defense of his family as well as his country. The family is, after all, a unit of a total society. It never exists as an isolated entity. A man cannot rightfully, however, introduce any new member into this covenant if that person will disrupt the family unit.

This principle of the covenant of intimacy should extend as well to financial support. A man cannot deprive his family of the necessities of life in order to provide for aging parents. Most primitive tribes have recognized this principle, although it was often the older people in those tribes who insisted that the principle be observed. We are seldom confronted today with the problem of depriving our children of food in order to help the grand-parents. We usually meet this problem in the difficult decision as to what is necessary for life. Are TV, a washing machine, a new car, a vacation trip, etc., necessities? Most families can provide help for grandparents without cutting into real necessities, but most of our necessities are what used to be called luxuries. We can usually make many more sacrifices for grandparents and neighbors than we dream of making. Nevertheless, the fundamental principle still holds that a man is responsible to the family unit which is created through the covenant of intimacy.

Our problem is that we do not know what the grandparent will do to the covenant of intimacy. We cherish our privacy. This is our home. The idea of introducing a parent-in-law raises all kinds of questions. However, this grandmother may bring new relationships, a spread in intimacy, a refreshing change of atmosphere and many new gifts to the family. She may ease the way for the children by listening to their problems and telling them stories while mother is busy. She may free the parents for time off from the home. She may bring humor and objectivity into an overtense and overly intimate situation. She will undoubtedly bring much wisdom and counsel to the couple, if they are mature enough to ask her advice. How can Jane and John decide this question? How do they know that grandmother will disrupt the intimacy of the home? The grandmother may ease the pressures in the home and draw Jane away from too much preoccupation with her children. The principle still holds, but it does not free us from the decision in the light of concrete circumstances. It is probably true that many modern families would benefit by including a parent-in-law in the home as necessity arose. If couples feel that they cannot do this, however, they need not feel guilty. They have to make the decision with a real sense of responsibility for the family. If they can be certain that the grandparent will disrupt the marriage, they have no choice.

We need not feel unreasonable guilt over the fact that our kind of life does not allow for the three- and four-generation household. On the other hand, we pick and choose our neighbors with too little recognition of our responsibilities to those whom God has placed next to us. It is too easy to carry this same attitude over to our parents. We often avoid those relationships that disturb us, and we are able to do this today. We can move or make friends in another part of town. We can live as strangers in a block by ignoring our neighbors. This attitude is, at best, a rather irresponsible way to live. It is even more irresponsible in relation to our parents. We have inescapable obligations to all those whom God places next to us in life. This is particularly true of obligations to parents.

The practice of avoiding all disturbing relationships also deprives us of the growth which comes with facing difficult relationships. Most people are upsetting for us because they touch us at our weak points. They may reflect the things that we fear in ourselves. Some people are deeply troubled by cripples and others by sick people. These experiences often represent the fear of being crippled or being sick. People often disturb us because they represent the things we want and feel that we shall not have. We may be troubled by their religious faith, their freedom in spending money, their social position, or their good looks. These are very complex matters which should not be treated too simply, but it is true that we usually find the difficulty in ourselves when others bother us. If we have to live with these disturbing relationships, we have an opportunity to overcome many of these fears. If we can avoid such relationships, we can run away from ourselves all through life.

Our forebears had to live with many difficult relationships. They could not escape. We have no need and no desire to return to such a restricted way of life. We cherish the freedom to determine many of the circumstances of our lives. We run the risk, however, of avoiding personal growth and continuing with childish fears if we turn away from every difficult relationship. One might answer to this that work exposes us to enough difficult relationships without our having to face them in our family circle. At least we should be able to pick and choose among our neighbors. But the relationships at work can be kept at a reasonably mechanical level of co-operation. We do not aways have to become personally involved with our fellow workers. Thus, we avoid the personal encounters through which personal growth can come.

The decision about including a grandparent in the home is complicated by our habit of picking and choosing relationships. It is too easy to assume that grandmother will present difficulties and therefore must be excluded. Often grandmother will present problems which should have been faced long ago. Her reactions to the lack of discipline in the home may be a necessary corrective to the rule of the children. Husband and wife may well be afraid of discipline because of their own resentments against their upbringing. These resentments are now being passed on through avoidance of any discipline. There is no way out of this unless a new relationship enters the picture and upsets the balance. Most of us need difficulties and conflicts if we are to face our real weaknesses. Growth is always a painful process and can be extremely difficult when our personal attitudes are in question. These are some of the gains which need to be considered as we face the question of including older people in the home. It may not be easy, but it may mean a new life for the family.

Many simpler societies have had to leave their old folks to die. The pressures to survive were too great to allow for extra persons who could not carry their weight. One gets the impression that the older people insisted on being left. The younger people felt obligations to their parents and felt guilty about leaving them. Many of us have moved to a standard of living which can provide for both older and younger people. We are not pressed for survival. We are troubled most by our personal relationships. In this situation many older people prefer to remain alone in order to protect their children's marriages. They too prefer to perish rather than jeopardize the new family. We have the same problem as simpler societies, but now it centers on personal rather than physical survival. It is easier, however, to see whether there is enough food to feed eight or ten than it is to determine the effect of another person on an intimate group. Every intimate group tends to become exclusive. A new person is automatically seen as a threat. Nevertheless, the personal survival of an older person is often at stake in a decision like this. We have to be quite certain that this older person will wreck the home before excluding her from the family circle. The grandparent will tend to stay alone, if it is possible. Grandparents know some of the difficulties of bringing in-laws into a home. In staying alone, however, they may be choosing personal death. Such a choice can only be allowed if the personal survival of the intimate family is at stake.

There are, of course, many compromise solutions to this dilemma which need not be discussed. Many couples have supplemented the income of a grandparent in order to provide independence and freedom to visit.

Others have arranged for grandparents to live in the neighborhood. There are many compromises which can achieve realistic adjustments. No matter what the solution, the loneliness of older people is the pressing question which the intimate family has to face.

If a couple decides to include a grandparent in the home, there are additional problems to be considered. It seems fair to say that the personal question is the really crucial issue, but this is not the only consideration.

We have already mentioned the difficulty of financing a terminal illness. In our credit economy, very few families are in a position to carry such an expense. This can be a source of anxiety to the couple and to older people as well. In many cases, of course, older people die without prolonged illness. Furthermore, men and women in middle life can be stricken by prolonged illness. Nevertheless, the chances are increasingly high that older people will suffer from diseases which require months of hospital care. Perhaps we should consider adding medical coverage to old-age and social security provisions. Older people are seldom in a position to finance heavy medical expenses. They no longer have the future earning power with which to secure loans and indebtedness. If they have saved some money, it is soon gone with laboratory fees, doctors' bills, and hospital charges.

There is, to be sure, much resistance on the part of the medical profession to government medical insurance. After the wrangle over National Health Insurance, hospitals and insurance companies have cooperated in the development of private coverage. The success of these plans is still undecided, since the costs of medical care have risen steadily. Many people have yet to be covered adequately for serious illnesses. There is certainly good reason to watch the growth of government activity in the sphere of personal life with some concern. The more such issues can be handled through private, local, and state authorities, the more personal responsibility can be maintained. On the other hand, matters like social security have to be integrated at a federal level in order to provide for movement of workers and inequalities in the income levels of various parts of the country. However the issue of medical coverage is finally decided, the protection of older people seems to fall legitimately within the social security provisions. Such protection would give reassurance to older people and would back those couples who wish to include their grandparents within the home.

There is also the question of financing the maintenance of an older person. We are not in a position to return to the thrifty virtues of early America. A collapse of credit buying today would mean financial disaster. Whether we like this development or not, it is now part of American life. This means that couples will soon be in a very poor position to take on an additional dependent. Our tax provisions now allow a regular deduction for each dependent. It may be that a somewhat larger deduction should be allowed for older persons. Families could be given financial encouragement to assist the older people or include them within the home. Precisely how much larger the deduction should be and just how much income the older person would need to disqualify him for the deduction is difficult to decide. Older people need a certain independence in return for their years of work. If their funds must go entirely for maintenance within the home, they will be living on handouts from their children. This is all right from the children's side in many cases, but it greatly restricts the freedom of the older person. One possible solution is a provision for tax deduction to cover older dependents at a figure nearer the real cost of maintenance.

The community can also back the family in its responsibility to older people by more intelligent planning of its suburbs and urban neighborhoods. There are still many old homes in the cities which can be fixed over for a family which includes older people. The trend, however, is to rebuild urban areas on the assumption that a couple will have two or at the most three small children. Families are finding it increasingly difficult to provide adequate housing for older people when they want to include them. One of the disasters of the postwar period in Europe has been the overcrowding of homes. Overcrowding breeds delinquency and is a menace to health. No responsible couple wants to endanger their children by such overcrowding. They will not be able to include older people unless city planning takes account of the family with more than two or three children.

The urban family can still make provision for grandparents to live independently in the neighborhood. City transportation is sufficiently adequate so that visiting back and forth is possible. This is often a better arrangement for grandparents who like their independence. Such an arrangement is impossible in the suburban developments. The suburbs have houses for different income levels, although they are mostly middle- and upper-middle-class homes. However, they make it difficult to include older people in the home. In fact, they are not designed for older people at all. Some developers have talked about older people settling down in later years in the suburb, but transportation problems and the pattern of life are designed primarily for young couples with small children. We are being saddled with a pattern of suburban life which automatically excludes older people both from the home and the community. Many couples have returned to the city from the suburbs to get away from this single age-group suburb. They miss the mixture of older, middle-aged, and younger people in their churches and associations. There is something artificial about being stuck with people of a single age grouping. It is like returning to adolescence.

The suburb has lost the counsel and stabilizing effect of older people. It has also excluded the older people from daily contact with the processes of life in the family. We have created a way of life in which it becomes increasingly difficult to keep contacts between children, parents, and grandparents. We feel guilty about what is happening to older people. Nevertheless, we let ourselves be pushed hither and yon by urban plans and commercial housing developments which do not necessarily take account of family interests.

These additional considerations of terminal illness, finance, and housing are not usually decisive on the question of older people in the home. Couples fulfill certain responsibilities to their parents in accordance with their maturity and sense of obligation. Most couples do the best they can whether other resources are available or not. These suggestions for governmental backing are simply ways of encouraging couples to overcome the personal isolation of older people. If we feel that it is sound to integrate the older generation into American life so far as possible, then we shall need policies which express this view. If we agree with the social agencies that older people can live happier and more useful lives within the home, then we can encourage couples to include them. No governmental encouragement can be a substitute for the personal capacity of the family to include older people. This will remain the fundamental issue in the personal survival of the older person. The intimate family does not lend itself to meeting this dilemma. Its exclusiveness is the source of both its strength and its problems. There is no easy way to include an older person in the intimate home, but mutual gains have accrued to those who have done it. Couples gain a certain freedom from their children through the help of an older person.

Children gain a new kind of relationship with a grandfather or grandmother. The older people find themselves caught up in the stream of life and often grow younger in the process. These are things to be encouraged in every possible way. They are not things, however, which can be legislated into existence.

A government protects and supports family life out of its own self-interest. The family contributes much more to the nation than could ever be requited in social security benefits. In fact, such benefits are merely the allocation of taxable funds which the family produces. Democratic government is only another name for the constitutional representatives of the total community of families. Fathers and mothers cannot allow their representative government to pre-empt their responsibilities without endangering the integrity of family life. This is an obvious word of caution when one begins to discuss governmental provisions for family security. Ultimately families must decide whether their methods of earning, saving, and spending can provide adequately for old age. If a credit economy makes such provision impossible, then social security becomes a method of saving for old age through taxation. This becomes a system of enforced saving. Then the question is how much must be saved to care for terminal illness and to provide some independence in later years. These are not decisions to be made by mysterious powers in some far-removed castle. They are basically family decisions. The family cannot make such decisions on the assumption that a beneficent power will produce these benefits through sorcery. These are family funds which must be allocated with full responsibility. The vitality and stability of a nation rests ultimately upon the integrity of its family life. The reverse, however, is also true. A family can only maintain its integrity in the kind of society which reinforces the responsible exercise of family duties. Any legislation to back family responsibilities for older people must be seen in the light of this two-way process. If we feel that our families should develop their responsibilities to older people, we must develop instruments which will make this possible.

It would be erroneous to suggest that older people are *a problem* today. Older people have specific kinds of problems in our society, but so do the other age groups. We have been concerned primarily with the relation of older people to their children and grandchildren in the home. This is actually one of the most difficult aspects of family life in our time. There are, however, many redeeming aspects to old age in our society which offset the family issue. Many older people are enjoying a freedom in retirement which they never knew in earlier years. They have been able to move into warmer climates, find new friends, and take the leisure for pursuits that they enjoy. They have been relieved of the grinding pressures of industrial, business, and professional work. Older couples have found time to develop their own companionship and mutual interests. They have been able to visit their children without having to share the cares of home and family. They have been able to indulge their grandchildren in ways in which they would never have dared to indulge their own children. They have traveled to countries which they had only seen on folders and travelogues.

The picture of old age in the U.S.A. is a very mixed one. There are still many isolated, lonely, and forgotten older people who need personal attention more than anything else. There are others who are still carrying many responsibilities and enjoying their work. There are others who are rejoicing in their quiet and freedom. We easily distort this mixed picture by concentrating on a particular problem such as family relationships. Nevertheless, the relationship of a child to his parents involves an intimacy which is not to be discarded lightly. In a Christian understanding of life, these relationships have an eternal quality. This means that they are to be worked through in mutual love and respect. Individual freedom from such intimacies is not to be gained by rejecting one's relationship to a parent, even though temporary rejections and conflicts may interrupt any human relationship. We are linked to our families and friends, as well as our enemies, for all time. We shall be brought to the full stature of our lives only in relationship to them. We are continually confronted in this life with decisions for and against our parents, friends, and enemies. These decisions are the inescapable meetings with God. In turning against our responsibilities to others, we turn against God who binds us to them in mutual love.

CHAPTER EIGHT

TIME FOR INTIMACY

The most virulent poison created by industrial society is excessive loneliness. Our way of life uproots people, carrying them upward or downward in the struggle for success. Human bonds are pulverized. Those who cling to family ties are soon left behind in the economic struggle. Those who press forward find themselves cut off from friends and associates. We are the uprooted. We are the producers of things and the servants of machines. We live with things, ideas, and prices. We rarely have time to live with people.

Human loneliness is not a new phenomenon. It is not even a bad thing in itself. All of us need to be alone at times. Many a housewife with small children would give anything to have a little time to herself. However, it is one thing to be alone in order to be quiet and recollect oneself. This is creative aloneness. We have too little creative aloneness. On the other hand, there is a kind of loneliness which comes from being isolated. We are not alone out of a desire for privacy. We are alone because our lives are not knit to other lives. We cannot share our hopes and fears with others, because we are bound in mutual support to no one. This is not creative loneliness. It is the estrangement of the isolated person who moves anonymously in the midst of crowds.

The breakdown of personal friendship is the clearest example of loneliness today. Friendships have usually filled the middle ground between family life and the less personal dealings of the larger community. Friends are bound together by common interests and experiences. They listen to one another and share their successes as well as failures. We still have friendships during school years, but they are left behind as job and marriage intervene. It takes time to develop friendship. We are too hurried to take this time. Friendships require continuing contact and association. We move too rapidly to maintain these contacts. Our way of life is not conducive to the growth of friendship. This middle ground of intimacy has almost disappeared in America.

Many would answer to this that they do have friends whom they see and enjoy. Their claim needs clarification, however, because the word "friend" has lost most of its meaning in our time. We have witnessed the transformation of friendship into affability. Everyone knows that Americans are friendly. We use first names after short acquaintance. We speak of Mr. Jones as a friend after having played one game of canasta with him. To hear us talk, one would think that we had scores of friends. Try and experiment at a social gathering some evening. Keep score on the number of names of friends that are dropped. The scores will be astronomical, particularly if the people who are gathered do not know one another very well. We have all played the game of "Do You Know" with new acquaintances. Most of the "Do You Know" people are intimate friends, if the other person does not know them. Casual acquaintances become friends overnight. Why? What has happened to friendship?

There is a simple explanation for this transformation. We are so uprooted that we have few if any friends. But life cannot be carried on without personal recognition and acquaintance. Even the company buyer must have some assurance that the supplier will fulfill the contract. A company cannot go to court over every purchase. We cannot sue every merchant who decides to pass up his guarantee on the refrigerator or stove. We need personal contact in the most commercial climate. We need personal confidence in others. Since most of us are anonymous in daily life, we must make contact—build personal ties. Friendship becomes a means of establishing personal contact which will undergird our agreements and deals. Very few people like the word "contact," but we know that modern commercial life would be impossible without it. The dealer is a contact before lunch and a friend after lunch. First names are soon used. Slap on the back! Next week we tell about our friend Joe, who handles this line.

This is the atmosphere of the lonely world of the uprooted. We have few real friends, but everyone is a friend. How many times has a new acquaintance asked you to stop in when you are going through Chicago or Dallas. Come in for a meal! Spend the night! We have lots of room! Try it some time. The man's wife would faint. This is not being cynical. The man is really sincere when he says this. He never pauses to think that he would be shocked if you did stop. This is a manner of speaking. This is being friendly. This is the world of affability which now passes for friendship.

The disappearance of intimate friendships would be no great loss if there were some substitute. There is nothing sacred about the idea of having friends. We do have some substitutes on the middle ground between family and commercial life. We have our clubs, associations, churches, and lodges. Here we meet "friends" with whom we have something in common. The marked growth of the churches in recent years may reflect this need for middle ground—for associates in an anonymous world. The rapid growth of churches in suburban areas undoubtedly reflects this groping search for people whom we can know. Loyalties to church groups are the last shreds of acquaintance for the fast-moving, anonymous man of today. We are uprooted and repeatedly torn from the groups which have come to know us. We are strangers in the midst of crowds.

Is this necessarily a bad thing? Perhaps we are nostalgic or sentimental in reflecting on this lonely existence which our way of life creates. Can we not be content with the abundance of our economy and accept a little estrangement as part of the cost?

There are two fatal diseases which come from excessive loneliness. The estranged and isolated person develops deep fears. All human beings need assurance that they belong somewhere. They become anxious and fearful when they are isolated. They feel rejected and useless. Such fears have a strange way of turning into hates. The feeling of rejection can thus be blamed on others. The haters are usually the estranged and fearful. This fact is fairly well established. Loneliness is not a neutral thing. It is a frightening and frustrating experience which leads to bad feelings toward any group that can safely be attacked. A person tends to strike out at others when he is blocked or frustrated. This is a common experience. A child receives a spanking and goes next door to beat up the little neighbor. There is no more frustrating experience than excessive loneliness. Excessive isolation and loneliness create bigots and experts in hate. Our deep racial and religious tensions today are in no small part the consequences of personal isolation.

Excessive loneliness also drives persons to join any group that will accept them. We see this most vividly in the teen-ager who joins a gang to overcome his feelings of isolation. If the gang is firing on the neighbors, he may pick up a gun in order to belong. The estranged and lonely are easily drawn into totalitarian movements that will promise them a place. We saw this in Nazi Germany. We have seen it repeatedly in totalitarian movements. The lonely and estranged lose all sense of discrimination. They search for a group that makes them feel safe and at home. After all, Big Brother does promise to take care of his own. He demands some rather unethical actions and he requires unquestioning loyalty, but he promises to get rid of the "bad guys" and keep the world safe for the "good guys." Unfortunately Big Brother does not really care about persons, so the lonely person is liquidated when he is no longer useful.

These are some of the dangers of excessive loneliness for a society. Intense loneliness leads to hate and gathers the lonely into a fellowship of hate. In addition, there is the simple fact that loneliness is a painful experience. If loneliness were not so painful, men and women would not go to such lengths in order to overcome it. The body politic cannot afford to allow too much of this poison to circulate in its system. This is a dangerous poison. Recall, if you can, some of your deepest experiences of loneliness. This is not easy to do. The human mind erases such experiences very rapidly. They are too painful to be retained. Moments of complete estrangement are the most painful experiences of human life. They close the self in a suffocating chamber. Time extends endlessly. The whole mind and body is obsessed with its isolation. Many people experience such loneliness when they are in love. Separations cut through the person until he suffocates from his isolation. We experience this at the death of those we love. This is the real sting of death. We are cut off from part of ourselves and experience deep physical anguish. Intense loneliness is so painful that it undermines all capacity for rational action. Anything is to be preferred to this estrangement.

There is no complete escape from loneliness in human life. Only the naïve person imagines that he can anchor his life in a group or a relationship and end all estrangement. A person lives his own life. Others can never know fully how he feels or what he thinks. There is a fundamental loneliness in human existence that can never be overcome. We can draw close to other people and find support, but we cannot escape from the self that must lead its own life. In fact, a healthy person needs periods to be alone with this self and collect the fragments of experience. Here, too, death reveals a profound reality of human existence. A man dies alone, even though friends may stand with him through the experience. Each of us passes through innumerable experiences alone. Death is the final evidence of the fundamental aloneness of human existence.

After this has been said, it needs to be added that there are degrees of loneliness. Even though the basic loneliness of our lives cannot be eliminated, we can share intimate contacts with others which make our loneliness creative rather than destructive. Our society has narrowed the sphere of intimacy almost exclusively to the immediate family of parents and children. The family is now the principal antidote to the poisons of excessive loneliness.

Dilemmas of Intimacy

The strains in family life today can be attributed primarily to the narrowing of intimacy to the home. We have already examined many of these strains in an attempt to discern fruitful ways of handling them. We have noted the haste with which many are entering marriage and the desperate search for intimacy that surrounds romantic love. We have considered the difficulties arising from attempts to include older people in the home and the fearful loneliness to which many older people are now exposed. However, two kinds of tension seem to be paramount in the modern home. The family is torn between its need for intimacy and its need for authority to guide its life. The family is also caught in a difficult struggle to provide children with a sense of belonging that does not tie them too closely to their parents. Both of these dilemmas have arisen as the family has become the exclusive sphere of intimacy on the American scene.

The more intense the loneliness of husband and wife, the more difficult it is to develop a center of authority in the home. Personal intimacy and authority are contraries which always exist in tension. The stronger the personal need for intimacy, the more disturbing is the subordination to authority. Since people today are suffering from intense needs for intimacy, we can assume that very few families can tolerate much formal authority in the home. If the male authority is to be recovered in the modern family, it can only be done very slowly. The central job of the family is to provide a sphere of intimacy in which excessive loneliness can be overcome. This is its primary task. All other concerns must be subordinated to the accomplishment of this task. If we accept this fact, we can handle the problem of authority without undue haste and without doctrinaire claims that it must be such-and-such. A proper division of authority can only arise as a fruit of personal intimacy.

The conflict between authority and intimacy is clear from the nature of intimacy. An intimate relationship is a bond of mutual concern and support between equals. Two people stand together as equals in their concern for one another. No distinctions of ability, mental aptitude, riches, or office can be allowed to dominate an intimate relationship. These barriers may exist in other settings, but they cannot be allowed to operate in friendship or marriage. Barriers of inequality are excluded from consideration in intimate relationships. Persons bound together by mutual love and concern exist for one another.

Each will help the other and support the other. They counsel one another in difficulty and rescue one another in danger. These are the qualities of an intimate relationship. The intimate relationship assumes an equality as persons. However unequal the persons may be in ability, they are simply persons in their intimacy.

Authority, on the other hand, introduces inequality. Authority can only be exercised when one person subordinates himself to another on a particular matter. Let us picture the situation on the *Titanic* at the time of the tragic sinking. Husband and wife are on deck. The wife wants to stay with her husband. They have children at home. They resist the idea of being separated in this catastrophe. The husband insists that the wife enter the lifeboat and return to the children. In this crisis the husband exercises an authority to which the wife subordinates herself. In this decision they are not equal. So long as husband and wife agree, there is no issue of subordination and matters can be settled by consensus. When they disagree on critical issues, authority introduces a problem of subordination and inequality.

It seems desirable that wives encourage their husbands to take a more authoritative role in the home. Their husbands have been forced out of the home situation by the circumstances of modern life. Such a recovery of male authority is bound to upset the equality of intimacy. It need not threaten the intimacy, if husband and wife feel assured of the mutual concern in their relationship. This suggests that the real issue to be worked through is the personal intimacy of the relationship. If the personal bond is soundly established, allowing room for privacy and a sense of support, then the division of authority may follow. On the other hand, many couples cannot deal with their personal intimacy because the power struggle has frustrated both of them. The modern family will undoubtedly lean toward equality and intimacy no matter how chaotic the home becomes. It is the nature of loneliness to demand its due at any cost. Nonetheless, full intimacy cannot develop in a chaotic home that is ruled by children. At the risk of disturbing equality and arousing conflict, the problem of authority will have to be faced for the long-range good of the family. There is no great danger of undue inequality if the biblical injunction, "be subject one to another," is kept in mind and put into practice. This is the ground of equality on which intimacy rests. Husband and wife will differ in their abilities, interests, and responsibilities. Despite these differences, they are joined as equals in the covenant of intimacy. Every inequality in marriage is subordinate to this fundamental equality. The two have become one flesh.

The need for intimacy also creates tensions between parents and children. We have considered some of these difficulties. Such strains reflect additional problems of equality and inequality in intimate relationships. A fully intimate relationship is a person-to-person response between those who stand together in their personal life. At moments of deep intimacy, the persons shed the inequalities and differences. We occasionally experience such moments of intimacy across the barriers of inequality. A foreman and a worker may experience such a personal encounter. These are moments when the responsibilities of our particular jobs are set aside and the fullness of our equality as persons takes the foreground. Then the work of life continues and we don our inequalities once again.

Parents treasure moments of full personal intimacy with their children. They cannot, however, fulfill their responsibilities to the children if they expect intimacy to be the normal state of affairs. Children are not equal to parents in the order of family life. If they were, the parents could not protect and guide them as they mature to full personal responsibility. Our deep needs for personal intimacy tempt us to transgress the inequality between parent and child. We want to draw children into more intimacy than is proper. We treat them as equals, when they need the protection of an unequal, parent-child relationship. Our own need for intimacy seduces us into excessive intimacy with children. The children cannot meet these excessive demands, so we reject the children.

Inequalities separate us in life, but they also protect us from unfair competition. No one expects a student to compete with his teacher on an examination. A child is exposed to emotional demands which he cannot meet when he is drawn into intimacy as an equal. A child is also forced to fulfill obligations as an adult when he is treated as an equal. The transgression of the inequality of the parent-child relationship leads to excessive intimacy with children and makes them overly dependent. Ultimately it destroys their confidence in themselves. It also destroys their confidence in a protective and competent parent who can assure the stability of the world into which they are growing.

The need for intimacy in our time makes it difficult for parents to walk this narrow line between personal intimacy with children and protective authority over them. It takes great skill to be a parent in our day, since the modern home carries the full burden of personal intimacy for our society. The capacity of parents to maintain this tension between personal intimacy and realistic discipline is the most important parental skill in modern family life. The remarkable fact about the modern home is the success with which so many parents are executing this difficult job.

Personal intimacy has always had a place in family life. Human beings have always married for companionship and mutual support. Intimacy is not peculiar to the modern family. However, intimacy was formerly a secondary aspect of family life. If the family did not provide satisfying intimacies, there were always other relationships in which persons could find satisfaction. This middle ground between family and commercial life has been narrowed and impoverished. There are very few intimacies which can provide alternatives to an unhappy family situation. The alternative spheres of intimacy are too transitory in a rapidly changing social scene. Even friendship has become a rare experience. Personal intimacy is no longer one aspect of a family's business. It is now *the* business of family life.

The Promise of Intimacy

There is no crystal ball in which we can discern the prospects for this intimate family of our time. There is an unquestionable growth of interest in the family and concern for the home. There has been a steady rise in home-owning for some years. Men and women are marrying at an earlier age. The birth rate has achieved a steady and vigorous level. Home-owning and bearing children are both votes of confidence in family life. Divorce figures, by contrast, are rather frightening on the surface. They are not, however, quite so devastating as they look. The much discussed rise in the rate of divorce over fifty years has come largely from the tendency to legalize most, if not all, marital arrangements. These figures are also augmented by the freedom for women to escape impossible marital situations. The family today is not much less stable than the family of a few generations ago. In view of the strains in the intimate home, this suggests that more effort may be going into making a stable home than was necessary in earlier periods. Moreover, men are giving more time to their homes than was customary in earlier American or European life. We have discussed the battle fatigue suffered by so many women in the intimate home, but very few turn voluntarily from the intimacy of marriage to the business world. Children seem more rebellious today, although it is difficult to gain an adequate picture of child-rearing in earlier times. Delinquency rates certainly indicate an intensifying of rebellion among the young. On the other hand, children are dependent on their parents until a much later age because of the increasing pressure for education. Such prolonged dependence is bound to generate strains. On the whole, the balance sheet for the intimate family looks reasonably good. The pressures of loneliness in our society have driven men and women to exert more time and effort on the intimacy of family life.

We seem to be entering an era of family living such as our society has not experienced. Family life is gaining rather than losing importance. This is, perhaps, an optimistic assessment of the situation but most of the evidence points in this direction. Lifelong intimacy in marriage is one of the chief concerns of most young people. In a "lonely crowd," to use David Riesman's phrase, men and women want time for intimacy.

The resurgence of family life reaffirms certain personal values which our society has long neglected. For example, loyalty in personal relationships has suffered under the pressure to succeed. Stress on achievement has tended to depreciate the inherent worth of persons. The continuity of friendship and relationship has been broken by the changing character of urban life. Local community has been weakened by the spread of huge metropolitan areas. These and other personal values have been pulverized by the pressures of industrial society. The concern for family life is a protest against this annihilation of personal community. The intimate family affirms the pre-eminent worth of persons. It balances the impersonality of industrial society with an experience of personal intimacy.

If the new family merely counteracted urban impersonality through its personal life within the home, the prospects for urban life would be dim. This would mean relegating economic, political, and communal associations to increasing impersonality. However, the family seems to be thrusting beyond the home in its development of personal community. We see examples of this outward thrust in neighborhood development and religious interest. On the industrial side, there is a corresponding development of concern with the personal relationships in factories and offices. Our political parties continue to struggle with the growing impersonality of political organization which has come through the growth in population. The concern with personal community is not confined to the family, but it has found its natural center in the modern home.

It has become increasingly clear that personal integrity and responsibility are crucial elements in every human enterprise. This is true for families, research laboratories, industries, and nations. There are no substitutes for these human values. They cannot be replaced if they are not cultivated in the early years of life. Personal integrity and a sense of responsibility grow slowly through personal contacts in family and community. They are not the products of propaganda. They cannot be bought and sold in the market place. The family is now devoting all of its energies to the cultivation and support of these personal values. It is likewise thrusting this concern upon the schools, churches, neighborhoods, and local communities. As the family extends the sphere of personal community beyond the home, it will begin to reshape and humanize our cities and industrial areas.

OTHER ANCHOR BOOKS OF INTEREST

SOCIOLOGY

ALLPORT, GORDON W. The Nature of Prejudice, A149

BARTH, KARL Community, State and Church, A221

BENDIX, REINHARD Max Weber: An Intellectual Portrait, A281

BROWN, ROBERT MCAFEE, & WEIGEL, GUSTAVE, S.J. An American Dialogue, A257

CABLE, GEORGE W. The Negro Question, A144

CHEVALIER, MICHAEL Society, Manners and Politics in the United States, A259

DOLLARD, JOHN Caste and Class in a Southern Town, A95

FORTUNE, EDITORS OF The Exploding Metropolis, A146

GOFFMAN, ERVING Asylums: Essays on the Social Situation of Mental Patients and Other Inmates, A277

————— The Presentation of Self in Everyday Life, A174

GRANICK, DAVID The Red Executive: A Study of the Organization Man in Russian Industry, A246

HANDLIN, OSCAR The Newcomers, A283

————— Race and Nationality in American Life, A110

HERBERG, WILL Protestant-Catholic-Jew, A195

HOOVER, EDGAR M. & VERNON, RAYMOND Anatomy of a Metropolis, A298

MARTINEAU, HARRIET Society in America, Ed. Lipset, A302

NEGLEY, GLENN & PATRICK, J. MAX, eds. The Quest for Utopia, A326

PETERSEN, WILLIAM American Social Patterns, A86

RAAB, EARL, ed. American Race Relations Today, A318

RIEFF, PHILIP Freud: The Mind of the Moralist, A278

RIESMAN, DAVID Constraint and Variety in American Education, A135

————— Selected Essays from Individualism Reconsidered, A58

SCOTT, GEOFFREY The Architecture of Humanism, A33

SIGAL, CLANCY Weekend in Dinlock, A269

SOMERS, HERMAN & ANNE Doctors, Patients and Health Insurance, A309

VICO, GIAMBATTISTA The New Science of Giambattista Vico, Trans. Bergin & Fisch, A254

VIDICH, ARTHUR J., & BENSMAN, JOSEPH Small Town in Mass Society: Class, Power and Religion in a Rural Community, A216

WHYTE, WILLIAM H., JR. The Organization Man, A117

WIENER, NORBERT The Human Use of Human Beings, A34

WILLIAMS, RAYMOND Culture and Society, 1780–1950, A220

OTHER DOLPHIN BOOKS

OF GENERAL INTEREST

Yellow

ALEXANDER, HENRY   The Story of Our Language, C383
AUGUR, HELEN   Zapotec, C 81
BAGEHOT, WALTER   The English Constitution, C 241
BESTON, HENRY   Herbs and the Earth, C 271
BIERCE, AMBROSE   The Devil's Dictionary, C 225
BOVET, THEODOR   A Handbook to Marriage, C 23
BROOKS, JOHN   The Seven Fat Years, C 331
BULFINCH, THOMAS   The Age of Fable, C 132
CARTER, RICHARD   The Doctor Business, C352
DARWIN, CHARLES   The Origin of Species, C 172
DENHOF, WILLIAM C.   Popular U. S. Stamp Album (Magnum), C350
EDITORS OF *Fortune*   The Executive Life, C 69
FROMME, ALLAN, Ph.D.   The ABC of Child Care, C 95
FOWKE, EDITH and JOE GLAZER   Songs of Work and Freedom, C 240
GLAZER, JOE and EDITH FOWKE   Songs of Work and Freedom, C 240
GRAY, MADELINE   The Changing Years: The Menopause without Fear, C 242
HAGGIN, B. H.   Conversations with Toscanini, C 85
HECHINGER, FRED M.   The Big Red Schoolhouse, C361
HOFFMAN, JOSEPH G.   The Life and Death of Cells, C 156
HOLDER, GEOFFREY, with TOM HARSHMAN   Black Gods, Green Islands, C 235
LEONARD, RICHARD ANTHONY   The Stream of Music, C358
MACE, DAVID and VERA   Marriage East and West, C 161
MARRIOTT, ALICE   Greener Fields, C385
MYERS, C. KILMER   Light the Dark Streets, C 193
PATAI, RAPHAEL   Sex and Family in the Bible and the Middle East, C 40
PIKE, JAMES A.   The Next Day, C 272
ROSS, LILLIAN   Picture, C390
SACKVILLE-WEST, V.   A Joy of Gardening, C 220
STEWART, GEORGE R.   American Ways of Life, C 90
VERISSIMO, ERICO   Mexico, C327
WEYER, EDWARD, JR.   Primitive Peoples Today, C 200
WINTER, GIBSON   Love and Conflict: New Patterns in Family Life, C 279

DOLPHIN REFERENCE SERIES

AMERICAN GEOLOGICAL INSTITUTE   Dictionary of Geological Terms, C360
CARTMELL, VAN H.   Plot Outlines of 100 Famous Plays, C400
COPELAND, LEWIS (Ed.)   Popular Quotations for All Uses, C201
DE GOUY, LOUIS   The Gold Cook Book, C 202
FROST, S. E., JR.   Basic Teachings of the Great Philosophers, C398
FULLER, EDMUND   2500 Anecdotes for All Occasions, C 191
GOODMAN, ROLAND A.   Plot Outlines of 100 Famous Novels, C309
KIERAN, JOHN (Ed.)   Poems to Remember, C 99
MALLERY, RICHARD D.   Grammar, Rhetoric and Composition for Home Study, C381
ROSSMAN, I. J., M.D. and DORIS R. SCHWARTZ, R.N.   The Family Handbook of Home Nursing and Medical Care, C 141
SCHWARTZ, DORIS R., R.N. and I. J. ROSSMAN, M.D.   The Family Handbook of Home Nursing and Medical Care, C 141
SIMON, HENRY W.   100 Great Operas and their Stories, C 100
WITHERSPOON, ALEXANDER M.   Common Errors in English and How to Avoid Them, C382

OTHER DOLPHIN BOOKS

DOLPHIN HANDBOOK SERIES

ALEXANDER, MARY JEAN Decorating Begins With You, C354

BARR, STRINGFELLOW and STANDARD, STELLA The Kitchen Garden Book, C359

BLANCH, LESLEY Around the World in Eighty Dishes, C 298

BRUNNER, LOUSENE ROUSSEAU Magic With Leftovers, C362

CANNON, POPPY The ABC's of Quick and Glamorous Cooking, C348

CRAWFORD, JOHN R. How to Be a Consistent Winner in the Most Popular Card Games, C 180

EMBURY, DAVID A. The Fine Art of Mixing Drinks, C 177

FERGUSSON, ERNA Mexican Cookbook, C 312

FLESCH, RUDOLF A New Way to Better English, C 214

FINE, BENJAMIN and LILLIAN How to Get the Best Education for Your Child, C380

FOLLETT, BARBARA LEE The Check List for a Perfect Wedding, C 341

HIBBITT, GEORGE W. How to Speak Effectively on All Occasions, C 310

JOHNSON, WENDELL Stuttering and What You Can Do About It, C349

JONES, CANDY Make Your Name in Modeling and Television, C 222

LEVERTON, RUTH M. Food Becomes You, C 266

LEVINSON, LEONARD LOUIS The Brown Derby Cook Book, C317

LONDON, ROBERT and ANNE Cocktails and Snacks, C366

MC GUIRE, LELIA Old World Foods for New World Families, C 280

MACGOWAN, KENNETH A Primer of Playwriting, C365

MARGOLIS, ADELE P. Pattern Wise: How to Make and Use a Basic Pattern, C 203

MAUROIS, GERALD Cooking with a French Touch, C 184

MORRIS, WILLIAM It's Easy to Increase Your Vocabulary, C 215

POSTGATE, RAYMOND The Plain Man's Guide to Wine, C 330

POWERS, DAVID GUY How to Say a Few Words, C 178

REINFELD, FRED A Chess Primer, C395

——— Complete Book of Chess Tactics, C143

RITOW, IRA Capsule Calculus, C336

ROOSEVELT, NICHOLAS Creative Cooking, C 213

RULE, COLTER, M.D. A Traveler's Guide to Good Health, C 218

SANDLANDS, GILLIAN Salads for the Gourmet, C 253

STANDARD, STELLA Whole Grain Cookery, C342

STANDARD, STELLA and BARR, STRINGFELLOW The Kitchen Garden Book, C359

TIMES OF LONDON The London Times Cookery Book, C194

WALDO, MYRA Beer and Good Food, C 196

WARREN, ANN Modern Guide to House Plants, C368

WASON, BETTY Dinners That Wait, C353

WATKINS, A. M. Buying or Building the High Quality House at Lowest Cost, C374

WILLIAMS, ROGER J. Nutrition in a Nutshell, C396

OTHER ANCHOR BOOKS OF INTEREST

GOVERNMENT AND POLITICAL SCIENCE

ARON, RAYMOND On War, A171
BARKER, ALAN The Civil War in America, A274
BROGAN, D. W. Politics in America, A198
BULLITT, STIMSON To Be a Politician, A264
CHEVALIER, MICHAEL Society, Manners and Politics in the United States, A259
FROMM, ERICH May Man Prevail?, A275
HAHN, WALTER F. & NEFF, JOHN C. American Strategy for the Nuclear Age, A224
HANDLIN, OSCAR Race and Nationality in American Life, A110
HEARD, ALEXANDER The Costs of Democracy, A288
HOOVER, CALVIN B. The Economy, Liberty and the State, A241
KIMBLE, GEORGE H. T. Tropical Africa: Land and Livelihood (Vol. I), A303a
————— Tropical Africa: Society and Polity (Vol. II), A303b
KISSINGER, HENRY A. Necessity for Choice, A282
————— Nuclear Weapons and Foreign Policy, A152
LETWIN, WILLIAM, ed. A Documentary History of American Economic Policy Since 1789, A280
LIPSET, S. M., TROW, M. A. & COLEMAN, J. S. Union Democracy, A296
LUBELL, SAMUEL The Future of American Politics, A71
MARX, KARL, & ENGELS, FRIEDRICH Basic Writings on Politics and Philosophy, A185
MILLER, PERRY, ed. The Legal Mind in America, A313
NEGLEY, GLENN & PATRICK, J. MAX, eds. The Quest for Utopia, A326
NEHRU, JAWAHARLAL The Discovery of India, A200
PIERSON, GEORGE W. Tocqueville in America (Abridged), A189
ROOSEVELT, JAMES, ed. The Liberal Papers, A290
TOCQUEVILLE, ALEXIS DE The Old Regime and the French Revolution, A60
WILSON, EDMUND To the Finland Station, A6

PSYCHOLOGY

ALLPORT, GORDON W. The Nature of Prejudice, A149
BETTELHEIM, BRUNO Paul and Mary: Two Case Histories from *Truants from Life*, A237
BRENNER, CHARLES An Elementary Textbook of Psychoanalysis, A102
FREUD, SIGMUND The Future of an Illusion, A99
————— A General Selection from the Works of Sigmund Freud, Ed. Rickman, A115
FROMM, ERICH May Man Prevail?, A275
GOFFMAN, ERVING Asylums: Essays on the Social Situation of Mental Patients and Other Inmates, A277
————— The Presentation of Self in Everyday Life, A174
JONES, ERNEST Hamlet and Oedipus, A31
JUNG, C. G. Psyche and Symbol, A136
RIEFF, PHILIP Freud: The Mind of the Moralist, A278
VICO, GIAMBATTISTA The New Science of Giambattista Vico, Trans. Bergin & Fisch, A254
WHYTE, LANCELOT LAW The Unconscious Before Freud, A286
WIENER, NORBERT The Human Use of Human Beings, A34

OTHER DOLPHIN BOOKS

PHILOSOPHY AND RELIGION

Red

ARNOLD, EDWIN The Light of Asia: The Life and Teaching of Gautama, C 289

AURELIUS, MARCUS The Meditations of Marcus Aurelius (George Long, Trans.), C 68

BENTHAM, JEREMY The Utilitarians, C 265
    (JEREMY BENTHAM: Principles of Morals and Legislation; JOHN STUART MILL: On Liberty *and* Utilitarianism)

BERKELEY, GEORGE The Empiricists, C 109
    (JOHN LOCKE: An Essay Concerning Human Understanding (abridged); GEORGE BERKELEY: A Treatise Concerning the Principles of Human Knowledge *and* Three Dialogues; DAVID HUME: An Enquiry Concerning Human Understanding *and* Dialogues Concerning Natural Religion)

DESCARTES, RENÉ The Rationalists, C 82
    (RENÉ DESCARTES: Discourse on Method *and* Meditations; BENEDICT DE SPINOZA: The Ethics; GOTTFRIED WILHELM FREIHERR VON LEIBNIZ: Discourse on Metaphysics *and* The Monadology)

FOX, FREDERIC (Ed.) A Calendar of Hymns (Magnum), C357
———— Songs of Two Christmases, C356

GRANT, ROBERT M. with FREEDMAN, DAVID NOEL The Secret Sayings of Jesus, C 163

HUME, DAVID A Treatise of Human Nature, C 305
———— The Empiricists, C 109
    (JOHN LOCKE: An Essay Concerning Human Understanding (abridged); GEORGE BERKELEY: A Treatise Concerning the Principles of Human Knowledge *and* Three Dialogues; DAVID HUME: An Enquiry Concerning Human Understanding *and* Dialogues Concerning Natural Religion)

JAMES, WILLIAM The Varieties of Religious Experience, C 71

KANT, IMMANUEL Critique of Pure Reason (F. Max Muller, Trans.), C 340

LEIBNIZ, GOTTFRIED WILHELM FREIHERR VON The Rationalists, C 82
    (RENÉ DESCARTES: Discourse on Method *and* Meditations; BENEDICT DE SPINOZA: The Ethics; GOTTFRIED WILHELM FREIHERR VON LEIBNIZ: Discourse on Metaphysics *and* The Monadology)

LEWIS, C. S. (Ed.) George Macdonald: An Anthology, C373

LOCKE, JOHN The Empiricists, C 109
    (JOHN LOCKE: An Essay Concerning Human Understanding (abridged); GEORGE BERKELEY: A Treatise Concerning the Principles of Human Knowledge *and* Three Dialogues; DAVID HUME: An Enquiry Concerning Human Understanding *and* Dialogues Concerning Natural Religion)

LONG, GEORGE (Trans.) The Meditations of Marcus Aurelius, C 68

LUCRETIUS On the Nature of Things (H. A. J. Munro, Trans.), C 80

MILL, JOHN STUART The Utilitarians, C 265
    (JEREMY BENTHAM: Principles of Morals and Legislation; JOHN STUART MILL: On Liberty *and* Utilitarianism)

PASCAL, BLAISE The Thoughts of Blaise Pascal (W. F. Trotter, Trans. C 231

PLATO The Republic and Other Works (Benjamin Jowett, Trans.),

RENAN, ERNEST The Life of Jesus, C 59

SCHOPENHAUER, ARTHUR The World As Will and Idea (R. B. Haldane J. Kemp, Trans.) C 335

SPINOZA, BENEDICT DE The Rationalists, C 82
    (RENÉ DESCARTES: Discourse on Method *and* Meditations; BENEDICT DE SPINOZA: The Ethics; GOTTFRIED WILHELM FREIHERR VON LEIBNIZ: Discourse in Metaphysics *and* The Monadology)

THOREAU, HENRY DAVID Walden, C 10